Y0-CAJ-737

 11/24
STRAND PRICE
$5.00

INSIGHT OUT

INSIGHT OUT

SORT-of POETRY

ELLEN AZORIN

Copyright ©2005 by Ellen Azorin
All rights reserved.

ISBN 978-0-9771073-0-8
ISBN 0-9771073-0-2

Published by Cantaloupe Press
157 West 79 Street, #4A
New York, NY 10024

Distributed by Cantaloupe Press
Tel. 212.724.2400
www.cantaloupepress.com

Library of Congress Control Number: 2005907433

For information regarding permission
to reproduce selections from this book,
call or write Cantaloupe Press
or e-mail:
information@cantaloupeproductions.com

FIRST EDITION

To Grandma Rose
who taught me the joy of
the act of creation,
and that this joy can be found
in anything from
the art we hang in museums,
to the artful arrangement of
a platter of tomatoes.

THANKS to every person who ever read
one of these and told me it made them laugh,
cry, agree, disagree, mull or remember.
Special thanks to Mom, Florence Fanshel,
Carol Butler, David Williams, Dionísio Santos,
Kenneth Feldman, Lili Rysz.

Contents

1. HERE AND NOW

2. DIRTY SNEAKERS

3. DAYLIGHT SAVINGS

4. COLOR CODING

5. SHARING JEWELRY

6. FATHER'S DAY

1. HERE AND NOW

HERE AND NOW

When I'm here and now
it seems for an instant
that no place or time
could ever be this vivid.
Until I pass through
to the next moment
in the next space,
and another here becomes now.
This is a maddening mystery to me.
I have sometimes tried
to capture the sensation
of this instant,
this surrounding,
this entirety of
sight and sound and movement.
I've tried to memorize a tree,
to mind-record the shout of a child,
to suck in the sensation
of warmth or cold,
to feel the mass
of a building to my right,
the swoop of a car to my left.
But here and now
moves into memory
swiftly,
inevitably,
irretrievably.
There simply is no force
that compares to the power
of being present
in the present.

DEVOTION

I get this tender feeling
every time I see a dog
parked patiently outside a store
waiting for someone to return.
Everything about him
is focused,
and no distraction
or diversion
will diminish his devotion
to his single-minded task.
I want to comfort him,
commend him,
assure him there's no need to worry.
I see in him so clearly —
in his eyes, his ears, his posture —
what I've often felt but try to hide:
that nothing will be right again
until the person I'm waiting for
is back again
for me to see
and hear
and smell
and touch
and be near.

GOD

After a lifetime of hardcore atheism,
I've decided I want to believe in God.
I've decided I like the idea of somebody,
albeit an amorphous somebody,
who loves me
and watches out for me
and takes care of me
and has the power to make things happen
even when I can't.
I have to make a real effort with this
because every fiber of my upbringing
shouts out that this is a ridiculous concept.
But a small voice inside me protests.
Damn, if other people can believe this,
why can't I?
Such a lovely idea.
It's worth working at.
So sometimes I concentrate and
smack down that nasty rational part of me
and make myself believe.
And I feel so comforted and protected.
I think for me, God is a memory.
Or maybe a wish.
God is everything I wished
my father could be
when I was a child.
And in allowing myself to believe,
I give myself my father.

WEATHER

As the first chill of New York
falls
upon us,
we walk around hugging ourselves
instead of each other.
Lids lower to shield our eyes from gusts
and we look at gray sidewalks
instead of people passing by.
I have tried with occasional success
to see the bright side of the thermometer,
the challenge of facing
and embracing the wind,
and climbing through
ice-crusted snowdrifts on corners
(sorry, no snowmen in my life).
I call forth thoughts of
crisp clean breathing and ruddy cheeks
instead of chapped lips and frozen fingers.
But I am a shivering whimpering
failure at this.
As I get out my stock of
scarves and gloves
and various other encumbering defenses,
the best I can honestly profess is
acceptance,
remembering the simple wisdom that
this too shall pass,
and life, like weather, has its cycles —
some more enjoyable than others.

AIRPLANE TIME

Airplane time is different.
Each minute has at least 70 seconds.
Every hour has about 100 minutes.
And while time gets longer,
space gets shorter.
Each foot has just 10 inches.
Other things on airplanes
also are transformed.
Food you would throw out at home
becomes edible,
even makes you ask for seconds.
You watch the worst movie in the world.
Gratefully.
Where at home, you get annoyed
if the toilet seat is left up,
in the plane you are thrilled
if it isn't left soaked.
I watch with envy those travelers
who settle in with a good book and
calmly turn pages all the way
from New York to Seattle.
My mind goes on stall
the minute my behind hits the seat.
Incapable of anything more challenging
than reading the headlines of the newspaper
the man in front of me is reading.
I eat.
I futilely attempt to sleep.
I squirm.
I crank.

[continued]

I let an hour pass.
Which of course in airplane time
is all of ten minutes.
[*Mommy, are we almost there yet?*]

CALM

I have been advised
by a friend who may possibly know
that in these moments
of feeling total turmoil,
I should try to remember
how it feels to feel calm.
This seems a simple idea.
Like sucking on a piece of chocolate.
But my mind is overwhelmed
by the fear in my chest,
and it's hard to call forth
those memories.
Were there ever times
when life seemed in order,
when I felt safe and protected,
and exactly where I was meant to be?
I go back in my mind,
hoping to answer,
with little success.
You see, right now I'm frantic and
unable to focus.
I'll have to try again
when I'm feeling
calm.

NO BIRDS

The birdfeeder is full.
It calls out with its seed,
standing tall on the deck,
like a flag for the flocks in the canyon.
But where are the birds?
I look out from the kitchen
for those darting small things,
those bright blue wings,
those occasional streaks of
cardinal red.
This is Austin winter.
Not a hint of avian activity.
I miss the delight of each flitting arrival.
I have heard of migration.
I never anticipated
my personal sense of
loss.

EMPTY SPACE

I live in awe of you people
who use every moment of every day.
You never lack for something to do.
Empty space is a concept that's
simply not part of your vocabulary.
So, for you folks who have
never experienced its impact,
here's a primer in empty space.
First, you must learn to distinguish
between taking a break,
which some of you call a vacation,
and true empty space.
Empty space is not
a brief interval of relaxing
between useful functions.
Empty space is a void.
It evokes feelings like panic.
Despair.
Isolation.
It hurts so much,
you'd do almost anything to avoid feeling it.
In fact, many people do almost anything.
Smoke cigarettes.
Eat.
Allow years to pass in ego-crushing jobs.
Stay in horrible relationships.
But the fact is, for some of us,
empty space is a bridge we must cross
to get from one foothold to the next.
Empty space must be more than tolerated.

[continued]

It must be respected.
Even embraced.
Because out of it comes
the most amazing growth of all.
If we can live through this painful void,
we unearth resources within us
we never knew existed.
Discover talents and abilities
forgotten since childhood.
Find ourselves doing things
we never dreamed of.
I have spent my life fleeing
from empty space,
but on those few occasions
when I've managed not to run,
I have never failed to be rewarded.
Tonight, as I sit here in empty space,
I find myself turning to write.

NOISE

Noise.
I know and don't notice.
Indoor sounds:
my computer and printer
droning subtly but steadily.
Street sounds:
not just the big bangs
that make me jump or just jumpy,
but the insidious undercurrent of the city.
Building sounds:
the structure breathing
as people move in and out,
elevators, doors, tiled floors.
Sounds of time passing, light glowing,
the waves of radios and tv shows,
the news that
"you've got mail."
Occasionally I will turn something off
and be startled by the impact.
Like the many things
we only notice when they
stop.

LATE

A strange force takes possession of me
in the last few minutes
before I'm supposed to leave
to get someplace on time.
All of a sudden,
I remember a phone call
I've been meaning to make all day.
Or I notice some dishes in the sink
that have to be washed.
Or I feel compelled to locate
some unimportant item
I misplaced last night.
Or I see something in the hallway
that belongs in the bedroom,
and just have to put it back.
Or decide to check my e-mail
just one more time.
Each of these activities
inevitably takes longer than I think.
And of course there's always
that last trip to the bathroom.
I hate being late.
But there seems to be something
even more uncomfortable
about being early.

EARLY

I am so often late,
that I'm taken aback
when despite my bad habits
I arrive with time to spare.
Time.
On time.
Ahead of time.
Untaken time.
Time to breathe.
Compose my thoughts.
Organize.
Prepare.
My appointment begins and
instead of losing the first five minutes to
fuss and confusion,
I am ready.
Calm and alert.
Like waking after a good night's sleep.
I ponder the worth of this state of
full presence
and weigh it against
whatever usually makes me
so loathe to leave my house on time.
An extra task accomplished.
A phone call answered.
Or the simple fear of arriving early
and having to be alone with myself
with nothing to do.
I promise to give myself
this gift of time more often.

[continued]

But here I am
remembering that promise —
sitting in a taxi,
trapped in traffic,
feeling the familiar tension.
And very late.

BUS

Why is everyone staring at me
from outside the bus?
I'm sitting at the window,
feeling perfectly normal,
but evidently
something is attracting attention.
My hair?
(It couldn't look that bad!)
My shirt?
(It's just my usual black.)
My sunglasses?
(Maybe I look like someone famous.)
I'm starting to feel
either very glamorous
or very paranoid.
Then it comes to me.
There must be one of those
outrageous underwear ads
on the side of the bus,
right below me.
How easy it is to forget
that the world has
other things to wonder at
besides me.

12 STEPS

This is not A.A.
It's another kind of anonymous
which I choose to leave
anonymous.
Because it doesn't really matter what it is.
We are all here for some behavior —
be it addictive, obsessive, compulsive —
that has humbled us into seeking help.
I sit in a circle with others like myself,
and all I have to do is
show up,
be honest,
and listen.
I may not be cured.
But I never fail to learn something.
There is so much wisdom in this room,
it makes me think that all you folks
who've never had to struggle
with anything anonymous
are actually missing out.
You ought to have the uplifting experience
of listening to people for over an hour
where nobody postures or pretends.
Where nobody gives advice,
or judges,
or attempts to fix anybody else.
We've learned we're not as smart
as we thought we were.
And that's the first step
to anything.

BIRTHDAYS

At what age do we stop wishing we were
older
and start wishing we were
younger?
Is there some signpost
that signals this moment in life?
Birthdays are monumental
at age one, two, three. . .
The anticipation of
candles, cakes and kisses,
all the fuss
around us,
creates an aura of excitement
starting with bedtime the night before,
and all through that artificially special day.
Years pass,
and we mark the rites of passage:
twelve turns into the teen of "thirteen".
Sixteen is sweet.
Eighteen and twenty-one are empowering.
The twenties hold no terror.
But there comes a year
(when was that year?)
a dark day indeed,
when we realize we're celebrating
a downward trend.
I've always marveled at
celebrations of aging.
A gala 50th birthday.
The gathered clan at 80.

[continued]

The young toasting 90
as an accomplishment.
I've never achieved
that degree of acceptance,
that existential peace some people reach.
What recipe results
in that birthday cake
upon which any number of candles
can sit and be lit
with a smile?

MOM

My mother is learning e-mail
at age 83.
This may not seem like a big deal,
but consider that in the next room
she's still using
a rotary telephone.
And that almost every
modern invention she has in her house —
from VCR to microwave oven —
was preceded by years of
"I don't want it, don't need it,
it's just one more gadget
to complicate my life."
But though she's stubborn,
my mother is a practical person
with an unfailing instinct for survival.
In the last ten years,
it seems like most of her friends
have died or fallen ill.
Including Mike,
the loving companion
she miraculously met
after the death of my father.
My mother sheds her tears
and moves on.
She told me she has decided
to have a computer,
not (god forbid) because
it has any intrinsic value,
but because she wants to

[continued]

live in the same world as her children.
Today, as I open an e-mail from her,
"had some problem starting   but worked d
it out. hope i didn't do any damage.
signing off   at 5:25   Love   Mom" –
I am thankful.
And proud.

WAIT

Is there anything worse than waiting?
I'm sure there is,
but right now, it escapes me.
I'm at the airport
where my three o'clock flight
is now being scheduled for five,
and the skeptical clan,
we cargo-to-be,
are camped out in chairs
coping in our various ways.
Laptops and cell phones
are distractions of choice.
Some read magazines.
Some stare into space.
I, who usually panic
at the prospect of being prisoner
in the cold confines of an airport,
am taking some solace
from being plugged in.
But now I've completed
my airplane project,
made my business calls,
and phoned a friend.
My resources are running out,
and my mind is starting to take in the fact
that I'm stuck, helpless,
at the mercy of weather
and traffic control,
in a place I really don't want to be,
for an amount of time I can't predict.

[continued]

Will they announce a further delay?
Will the skies suddenly clear and
we'll leave right away?
Should I pray?
How will this turn out?
The answer is forthcoming.
But I'll have to
wait.

FRAMED

I have my own private art gallery
hung on the facade of the
building across the street.
Inside each window frame,
a small scene.
I know the charms of each
like a museum buff knows
the paintings on the walls
of the Metropolitan Museum.
Woman In Red Apron Preparing Dinner.
Man In Striped Pajamas Shaving.
Still Life With Television.
And my favorite,
Man In Armchair Reading,
a simple composition, perfectly balanced:
a man bent over a book,
his white hair and shoulders
illuminated by a golden glow,
shades of Vermeer.
Day and night,
whenever I look, he is always there,
in exactly the same position.
So much so that I started to wonder.
Doesn't he ever go out?
Doesn't he ever get tired of reading?
The thought even crossed my mind,
maybe he really is just a painting.
But then one day
he reached for a cup of coffee.

GOT THROUGH

Sometimes I find myself thinking,
"Whew, got through that."
Got through New Year's Eve,
or some other occasion
of forced and unfelt festivity.
Got through that meeting I was dreading.
Got through that dinner
with a visitor from out of town.
Got through that doctor's appointment.
Got through a difficult task.
And then I catch myself.
When it's all over,
I'll have gotten through
my life.

SUBWAY MUSIC

The music's getting better and better
in the subway.
The acoustics are fantastic.
The audiences are not just captive,
but grateful.
These guys must be taking in
a decent day's pay,
judging by the number of fists
reaching into handbags and pockets
and coming up with dollar bills.
At Times Square, I've seen one quartet
that positions two players
on the downtown platform,
and the other two on the uptown side,
so their sounds bounce
forth and back across the tracks,
filling the huge vaulted space
with reverberations,
periodically drowned out
by ear-shattering din.
Here at 72nd Street down under,
a guy who sounds like Stevie Wonder
is at work with a trio,
his sweet, clear voice backed up by
keyboard, guitar and drums.
Now they're all singing *a capella*,
bopping and jiving
and livening up
this dreary platform.
Damn, here comes my train.

BLIND

Coming home from an appointment
and feeling a bit lost
about how to manage the rest of my day,
I ran into a blind acquaintance
on the subway.
He told me he was returning
from New Jersey.
Alone.
Yet he travels without a dog.
Just a little white stick
that folds up on itself when he's sitting.
I rode with him to his stop,
a complex express station,
and followed him in amazement
as he led me down and up
various staircases and corridors
until we reached the street,
using his extended white stick artfully
at critical moments.
He did not take my arm
as I walked alongside.
Only when we reached the curb
did he need any guidance,
and even this he accomplished deftly —
not with a gesture of dependency,
but putting his arm around my shoulder
as if protecting me.
We said our goodbyes
and he turned confidently
towards his home,
leaving me to wander.

GENEROSITY

There's a kind of generosity
I don't understand.
It's giving away more than you can afford.
The man is flat broke in Brazil.
Scrounging carfare and cigarette money.
As his few remaining dollars dwindle
with no reinforcements in sight,
the worst drought of the century
hits the north of his country.
Truck caravans are dispatched
from the capital.
The citizenry is called upon to contribute.
The middle class sits by
and bemoans it all on TV.
He goes to the neighborhood supermarket,
buys ten dollars worth of groceries,
and brings them to the local relief effort.
Help.

FALL BACK

Spring forward, fall back.
For months,
the sun has snuck out earlier each day.
But today we officially let him get away.
The pretty part of autumn is done,
leaving the trees' debris on sidewalks
like yellow slush after the rain.
Soon we will be lit by the gaudy glow
of bulbs strung and hung.
For now, just fall back.
An hour gained?
I feel the loss,
as I begin the descent into
the deep dark ending of the year.
I sigh and try not to wish it away.

CHRISTMAS

Mid November.
It's not even Thanksgiving
and already I'm hearing "Silent Night"
piped into the aisles
of a neighborhood store.
Who determines when Christmas begins?
There's something indecent about
decking the halls
before the last leaf falls.
Mid November.
We've just recovered from Halloween.
Let's pause.
Hold off a bit on Santa Claus.
Try to accept that life is okay
without naming it after a holiday.

DINNERTIME

The sun hangs like a cherry tomato,
ripening by the minute across the Hudson.
It spills its golden juices over asphalt streets,
illuminating the hordes
streaming out of subways and buses
with their backpacks and briefcases,
sore feet and loosened ties.
It's delivery hour on the Upper West Side.
Cross carefully:
the local restaurants
have sent forth
their immigrant brigades on beat-up bikes.
Flat pizza boxes perch atop wire baskets.
Szechuan chicken hangs on handlebars.
Paper bags are packed with
nachos and noodles,
comidas chinas y criollas
and gourmet Vietnamese.
On the sideswalks,
tired office workers,
heading for home,
stop in for take out.
Who's this handsome fellow
striding by with nothing but
a smile and a fistful of flowers?
Does dinner await?
Could somebody actually be home cooking?

TRANSPORTATION

I've always been fascinated by
self-propelled movement.
(Stepping on the gas in a car doesn't count.)
I remember this first when I learned to ski:
flying down the slope,
I was a passenger in my own body,
my mind and muscles doing their work
while I took the ride.
I've had this sensation while running:
relaxing into the rhythm
of footfall and breathing,
and simply observing the passing scene.
I feel it as I ride my bike in New York City:
here, where the hills are short
and almost effortlessly surmounted,
it's easy to forget
that my legs are in motion.
I glance to each side
as I glide through traffic,
slow down for the kids
bursting out of their school,
watch the people on the grass
as my bike climbs the path into the park.
I lean into the curves
as I circle the Great Lawn.
Suddenly I'm on the last lap,
emerging from the park,
and in a whoosh I'm at my door.
I savor the magic of my arrival.
I've been transported.

ZERO TOLERANCE

I choke every time I see
a mention in the newspaper
about an elected official's program of
"Zero Tolerance."
I was brought up to believe that
tolerance was a good thing.
Something you'd never
want to have "zero" of.
Tolerance.
The word itself was a lesson in
understanding.
Empathy.
Acceptance.
An effort to go beyond our own limitations
and see another point of view,
or culture, or circumstance.
No amount of rhetoric
about the war on crime
or the quality of life
will ever justify this distortion
of a beautiful word.
And a beautiful concept.

TERROR

As children,
terror was a bad dream.
Or the bogeyman coming to get you.
We told scary stories around campfires
and screamed on the rollercoaster.
As we grew up,
the word took on new meaning.
Terror was trembling at serious danger.
We learned it was
one of the most powerful emotions
in the spectrum of human existence,
as were joy,
and anger,
and love.
And we used the word sparingly.
But today it trips off our tongues
and our hearts don't skip a beat.
This terrible word,
which should be held in a cage
within our vocabulary,
is on every page,
every broadcast,
every world-conscious conversation.
Those in power play upon it,
toy with it and toy with us.
It has been unleashed
like the panic it promises.
Words matter.
Spare us this word.
Most of all,
spare us.

2. DIRTY SNEAKERS

DIRTY SNEAKERS

Enjoy the feeling.
Because it's only going to last
a very short time.
It may be five minutes.
It may be five days.
But as sure as the sun will set in the west,
your new white sneakers
will receive their first scuff.
You walk around that first day so proud.
And so damn vulnerable.
To tell the truth,
that first scuff is almost a relief.
The question is,
where do you go from here?
Here, the world divides.
There are those who never give up the fight.
They'd sooner go out in the street
with no underwear
than show their feet in dirty sneakers.
Then there are those of us
who from this point on feel,
"what's the use?"
The weight of perfection is lifted.
We walk without wincing through grass.
We kick doors that are stuck.
Ride bikes.
Day by day, the dirt sneaks up.
Until one day,
we look down and feel shame.
What to do?

[continued]

I have attempted on occasion
to wash my dirty sneakers.
Done research among
clean-sneakers people.
Skeptically obeyed instructions
to put them in the washing machine.
Removed and replaced the laces.
Stuffed them with paper as they dry.
I'm sorry, but you guys
must know something
you're not telling me.
Or you have wives or mothers with
secret tricks and techniques.
After all that work,
my dirty sneakers are still not clean.
Just less dirty.
It wasn't worth it.
Here's what I've decided:
I'm going to wear themdirty till they drop.
I have a spare pair in reserve
which I only wear on special occasions,
when I pretend they're as normal
as clean teeth.
The rest of the time, I'm free.
After all, what are sneakers for?

FRUIT SALAD

Every time I see one of those
fresh fruit combinations
outside a produce market —
so appealingly assorted,
so nicely sliced, so neatly plastic-wrapped
and nestled in a bed of ice —
I think,
oh sure,
you look so perfect and pretty
with your one luscious-looking wedge
of golden-ripe pineapple
perched on top to tempt me,
but underneath
you are rife with deceit.
I remind myself of
mushy past-prime honeydews,
the unsweetest picks of the cantaloupe crop,
and slabs of mealy, tasteless apples.
And then I think,
no, today will be different,
you will not disappoint me.
In fact, you look so delicious,
I'll be sorry when I've finished you,
so today I'll buy two.
No, Adam was not the
only sucker
to fall for fruit.

ICE CREAM

The terrier sits in perfect posture,
intent on the cup of ice cream
being held about a foot above his head.
He is rewarded with a spoonful of the treat,
his whole body lapping it up,
the sweet satisfaction evident
in every part from tongue to tail.
So motivated,
so focused is he,
not even another dog
passing practically under his nose
can draw his attention.
In between spoonfuls,
he simply waits,
eyes and stance unwavering.
What is it about certain foods —
what magic pleasure powers
do they possess —
that makes dogs of us all?

PEN

I can't be in a meeting without a pen.
And the person sitting next to me
always borrows it.
Just for a minute of course.
And never returns it.
This drives me crazy.
Being without a pen is like being naked.
Helpless.
To me, it's worse than kicking caffeine.
Suppose I have a really good idea
while some pompous but important idiot
is rambling on in the front of the room?
Or, on a less noble
but equally important level,
suppose I happen to remember
that I promised to call
my friend Elma this afternoon?
Or I think of something I need to pick up
at the market on the way home?
I'm forced to choose between
paying attention to the idiot
on the chance I may later be required
to have heard something,
in which case I risk forgetting my idea.
Or I can choose to hold onto my idea,
stubbornly shutting out all distractions
(like the proposed new marketing strategy
which I will shortly be required
to comment upon).
No pen.

[continued]

I'm lost.
While I pretend to pay attention,
my hands fumble desperately
around the bottom of my pocketbook.
My eyes sweep the conference table
in search of a writing implement
on the loose.
My neighbor meanwhile
sits happily beside me,
my pen poised upon his writing pad.
If I ask for my pen back, I'm being petty.
He'd never understand
how truly awful I feel without my pen.
Say, perhaps I ought to
write down these thoughts.
Now where the hell is a pen?

KEYS

In New York you need keys for everything.
To get in.
To get out.
To get wherever you're going.
Just to leave your apartment,
two are required,
upper and lower,
at least one of them Medeco.
In New York,
people like to lock themselves in.
Sometimes they unwittingly
lock themselves out.
Ride your bicycle —
you will learn the meaning of the word
Kryptonite.
(Two suggested if you want to find
not just your bicycle,
but both wheels attached when you return.)
Arrive at gym, open locker.
Leave town, car needs keys.
A day at the office?
Passkey, your office key, credenza key,
key to pee.
Home at last.
Jiggle one more in the building's front door.
Get mail.
Repeat from top.
There may be places on earth
where people have never seen a key.
Not New York.

[continued]

In fact, the thought comes to mind
that there may really be
a key to the city.

WRINKLES

What does the world have against wrinkles?
We don't seem to like them anywhere.
On clothes.
On skin.
We particularly don't like
a wrinkle in our plans.
As I ponder the question,
I wrinkle my brow,
which I'm sure is unattractive too.
What aesthetic despot
decreed that smooth
is preferable to creased?
That things should go smoothly.
Yes, smooth is definitely in.
But here I must end —
there's a matter I must
smooth over with a friend.

MULTIPLEX

At the Multiplex Theater
the multitudes are herded
into 12 large auditoriums
and it all works beautifully.
The line to buy tickets moves swiftly.
Sold-out shows are flashed on a sign.
One crowd pours out.
Another crowd files in.
At the refreshment stand,
we all move forward in orderly fashion
as truckloads of popcorn
are swooped into scoops
and measured into containers
("Are you really going to eat all that?").
The coke flows.
The candy goes.
The seats are comfortable.
There's enough room for your knees.
The sight lines are good.
There's never any garbage on the floor.
The sound is strong and clear
and it really does surround.
There are even almost enough
women's bathrooms.
There is great talent at work here.
Would someone please tell me
who is responsible
so I can vote for that person for Mayor?

MOVIES

Agreeing on a movie
to see with a friend
is a challenging and rewarding
activity in itself.
To start with,
it's almost a given that
your friend has already seen
the one movie you're really dying to see.
And vice-versa.
The negotiation begins.
First round:
I saw that one, friend saw that one,
I saw that one, friend saw that one.
Second round:
Not in the mood for a romance
(comedy) (foreign) (action) movie.
Third round:
My mother said it was awful,
the reviews were terrible,
I promised my boyfriend
(girlfriend) (cousin)
I'd go see that with him or her.
Fourth round:
It starts too early (too late).
I don't feel like going all the way
(downtown) (uptown).
Okay, you finally settle on something
neither of you really wants to see.
One of you gets there so late,
the only seats left are singles

[continued]

so you end up sitting separately.
As the trailers begin
and you sit alone among the couples,
you feel like announcing,
"but I'm not all alone on Saturday night,
I came with my friend."
And you wonder why
you went to all that trouble
to go to the movies together.

DOGS DO

Dogs squat
in the most ridiculous position
when they do their business
at the curb.
Their hind quarters sink down.
Their front legs brace.
Their ears strain back flat.
They hunch down their heads
as if they're shamefully embarrassed
to be doing this in public.
Poor creatures —
maybe they are.

DIRECTIONS

The family approaches you,
maps in hand,
the father looking both lost and shy.
You greet his inquiry
with your friendliest smile.
"Oh yes," you say,
"just go that way"
(you point helpfully)
"for three blocks"
(you hold up three fingers to make sure)
"then turn left"
(you indicate)
"and you'll find it on the right."
You feel so pleased to have been of service.
Proud you're such a knowledgeable native.
Surely you've undone the myth
that New Yorkers are a surly, unhelpful lot.
You watch them set out
on the course you instructed,
and satisfied,
you go on your way.
Three blocks later it occurs to you.
You made a mistake
and you've sent them
in the wrong direction.

SLEEP

It's so exquisitely pleasurable,
that seductive sleep
that creeps into your consciousness
like a narcotic.
Unfortunately,
it usually happens
when you can't appreciate it.
One of its favorite times, for example,
is during a business meeting.
You're sitting there perfectly alert
when out of nowhere
comes that slight dizziness behind your eyes
and before you know it,
your thoughts are floating off
on a fluff of cotton candy.
Or you're sitting in the theater
in your fifty-dollar seat,
trying to focus on the stage.
You feel the subtle sensation
as your brain begins to go limp,
melting into that syrupy,
semi-conscious state.
Your lids are heavy,
your chin is sinking downward,
you're sliding into submission. . .
then boom!
your head jerks upright
and you're in that awful desperate
struggle to stay awake.
This is perverse.

[continued]

Where is that sleep when we could
really delight in its deliriums?
The closest I've come to harnessing
this powerful natural phenomenon
is late-night television.
But this can be dangerous.
Every once in a while they fool you
and put on something
that catches your fancy,
and instead of drifting sweetly off to sleep,
you're up until 3 A.M.
And then the next day,
you're sitting in a business meeting,
when out of nowhere
comes that
slight dizziness
behind your eyes. . .

EYE EXAM

My face is pressed into an iron mask,
and I'm staring at letters from
"E" to . . . let's see.
I realize with a sense of failure
that I can't distinguish
the "C" from a "G".
Is that an "R" or a "P"?
The optometrist is asking:
"Which is better:
one. . . or two?
Two. . . or one?"
I'm trying to cooperate here,
but to tell the truth, they look the same
so I meekly ask him to repeat.
"Two. . . or one?
One. . . or two?"
By this time I'm embarrassed,
so I flip a mental coin
and decide to pick one.
(Or maybe it was two.)
He tries it again,
and I'm thinking he's trying to trick me.
Hey, it's hard to choose between
shades of no-good.
Am I being difficult?
Is "I can't tell the difference"
an acceptable answer?
This is an exam, and I'm doing my best, but
nothing seems to result in success —
not one. . . not two.

[continued]

Then just when I'm feeling blind as a bat,
he slips in a lens
and amazingly,
the world is back in focus again.
I get it now:
He wasn't testing my vision —
he was testing my faith.
Was blind,
but now I see.

NORMAL

In my vanity,
I harbor fears
about features
that don't measure up.
And in the typical fashion
of paranoia,
I think I must be
the only person on earth
with whatever it is.
Or at least I must have
the very worst instance of it.
Then I open the newspaper,
and see an ad for an entire business
devoted to correcting this condition.
I never make an appointment.
I don't need to.
It's enough to know
that I'm normal.

FRAGRANCE

I've arrived early for the concert
and am watching the crowd flowing in,
some bejeweled,
some bedraggled.
I'm feeling good
as I sit on my tuffet,
until little miss perfume
comes and sits down beside me,
wafting her fragrance my way.
It is a cloying stench,
and I fume at the fumes.
Soon there are others,
emanating from women
to my front and my back.
Now there is a cacophony of scent
like the orchestra tuning up onstage.
I'm writing laws in my head
(perhaps a constitutional amendment?)
banning all perfume in theaters and planes.
Fragrance is so personal,
how and why has it become so public?
You cannot close your eyes to shut it out.
Assaulted by aromas,
I make a serious effort to separate
what's happening to my nose
from what's happening in my ears.
I will save my anger for another day.
The music is glorious, and
I'm glad to report that the
Dvorjak
has doused the
Dior.

TEE-SHIRTS

One thing about tee-shirts.
You can never have enough of them.
And you always have too many of them.
Over the years,
they have gradually taken over my bureau,
and today it's time for a showdown.
We're looking at tee-shirts from
everywhere I've ever traveled
outside a 10-mile radius of New York City.
There are shirts from
every country my mother's visited
in the years since her retirement.
The ones that friends bring back
from vacation as gifts.
There are the ones I've gotten free —
and of course we all know
you never refuse a free tee shirt.
Shirts from the bank
and the hardware store.
For some reason,
I also have shirts emblazoned with
the logos of Maxwell House,
Velcro and Crest toothpaste.
Then there are the "event" shirts —
the ones given out at company outings
and 25th anniversary barbecues.
And the ones you buy
when you go to see an Indy car race
for the one and only time in your life.
And finally, there are the really rare shirts:

[continued]

the ones you buy because you like them.
The problem is what to do with them all.
Which ones do you part with –
the ugly ones?
Do you keep the ones that actually fit?
Or those huge ones that hang loose
and hide all?
As for the ones with sentimental value,
do they merit drawer space even though
they're faded and stained
but throwing them out seems like
an act of betrayal?
I really need to work this out.
Right now, even as I write,
my bed is piled high with my
lifetime collection and I'm
dealing with these difficult decisions.
Okay, I've decided.
Sentiment be damned.
I'm going for good looks.
Exotic places.
And a two-drawer limit.

NAIL POLISH

As the receptionist types my name
into her computer,
dispassionate,
disinterested,
distant,
I catch a glimpse of her nail polish.
It's the exact same shade
of highly modish
reddish-brownish
I agonizingly selected
just a few days ago at the nail salon.
"Say," I say,
"can I take a look at your nail polish?"
I extend my hand to meet hers in midair
and we both admire our collision of taste.
Now she's offering information,
like "it won't be long"
and "you're next."
You see, now we're pals.

SHOE SALESMAN

In the shoestore
I find myself unable to resist
the charm of this handsome young man
who makes me feel sexy
down to my feet.
He smiles,
playfully assesses my taste,
suggests, confirms, affirms.
It doesn't matter that I see him
doing the same with every woman —
young, medium and old —
in the store.
When he turns to me,
his attention is complete.
I know that in the hands of
an ordinary,
tired,
understandably exasperated shoe salesman,
today I would surely have walked out
empty-handed.
Instead I have two new pairs of shoes.
Sexy shoes.

PIN NUMBERS

I forgot my PIN number.
Actually, it's not my PIN number I forgot.
It's their PIN number.
Whenever possible,
whenever I have the choice,
I defy all accepted wisdom
about PIN numbers
and use a number transparently connected
to a simple fact about me
that any amateur thief
could uncover in five minutes.
Again defying all wisdom,
I use this same number on everything.
But they're tricky little fellows,
those banks and airlines and web pages
and telephone companies.
They've taken to assigning
their own PIN numbers.
Then you have to write to them.
Or call them.
And request that they change
their PIN number to your PIN number.
And then you have to remember
which ones responded
and which ones didn't.
Yesterday I tried to withdraw
some frequent flyer miles
for a trip to San Diego.
Sorry, wrong PIN number.
I swear I shuffled through

[continued]

my entire Continental Airlines folder
and tried three different numbers
from various correspondence
before I hit the jackpot.
I've had it.
So here, published and public,
in print and unforgettable,
is a complete list of all my PIN numbers
for all my money, mileage,
credit cards, phone cards,
web pages and e-mail accounts.
And just in case,
the last four digits
of my social security number
and my mother's maiden name.
No, wait a minute,
maybe that isn't such a good idea.

SINGLES

In the last week,
I have lost one glove,
one topaz earring
and one silver earring.
It's hardly the first time
I've lost one of a pair,
but I seem to be having
more than my share,
and the cluster of losses
has made me aware.
What to do with these
suddenly-single survivors,
who have no purpose all alone?
Should I stow them away
on the chance that their mates
may one day be found?
Or should I throw them out?
It seems too cruel —
I was so fond of them.
It's not fair that they have no value at all
simply because they're now one, not two.
But still, it's true.
Having come to this conclusion,
I nonetheless hang on.
Is this a testimony to my optimism?
Or simply evidence of my resistance
to accepting loss?
Wait. . .
just as I ponder this philosophical question,
here is my glove on the closet floor.

COUPONS

Coupons make me crazy.
I look for them in inserts.
I cut them out.
I save them.
All in the hope of saving 30 cents
on my contact lens solution,
or laundry detergent,
or frozen lasagna.
But my life has changed.
I no longer go shopping once a week,
armed with a list
and my coupon collection.
These days,
it's catch as catch can,
and I'm more likely to shop when
I happen to be passing the supermarket
on my way home from somewhere.
And of course at that moment
I'm not carrying my coupons.
So life goes on
and my coupons lie around
in a pile of optimism and potential,
growing dog-eared and wrinkled.
Until one day
I clean out my tote bag,
utility drawer or refrigerator door,
discover they've expired,
and throw them out.
With a feeling I confess
resembles relief.

SHOWER DOORS

After years of faithfully rolling
back and forth,
the doors in my shower
wouldn't slide any more.
This may seem small,
but taking a shower is one of those rituals
that can determine the course of a day.
And those sticky doors
were a daily reminder
of my powerlessness in the face of
mechanical invention.
What mysterious force had taken over?
I pushed and pulled and tried to figure out
why they worked when they did,
and why they wouldn't
now that they didn't.
Damn, I thought, who the hell do you call
to fix your shower doors?
I calculated the cost and inconvenience
of replacing them,
since the few times I've tried
to have things repaired,
I've ended up buying new ones anyway.
I was totally convinced
those doors were hopeless.
Here comes the amazing part.
On Sunday, I was seized
by an inexplicable inspiration
to do what men probably do
without thinking.

[continued]

I lifted the doors off their track
and took a look.
Well, well, well. Wheels.
Four little wheels,
attached to the top of the doors
with simple screws.
Their tiny rubber tires were worn out.
Feeling like Einstein,
I tucked one of them into an envelope.
Marched myself into a hardware store,
convinced this was just the beginning
of a long frustrating search.
Was flabbergasted to discover
that there exists a common item
called Shower Door Replacement Wheels.
Four for $2.49.
Went home.
Opened my toolbox.
Dug out one of those funny screwdrivers.
Replaced all four wheels.
Rehung doors.
I have returned to the bathroom
several times since to smile with delight
as I slide and glide them effortlessly
back and forth along their track.
I didn't give up, I didn't give in.
I win, I am rewarded.
Hey man, am I a genius, or what?

ANGER

If you're boiling over with
anger at your ex-spouse,
write a letter to the maker of
that much touted microwave miracle
you bought in a burst of belief.
(You'll easily find their address
on the package,
or these days a "www" where
you can simply click on "contact us.")
Tell them politely
that you think it's the
worst stuff you ever tasted,
and you want your money back.
If you do this right
(it may take some practice),
a few weeks from now
you will likely have a check
for the full purchase price,
along with a letter of apology
and several coupons –
no expiration date –
for any of their products
you'd like to try.
Try getting that kind of satisfaction
from your ex-spouse.

SUNGLASSES

On a Tuesday
I found the sunglasses in a taxi
and took them.
(Would you have?)
I later discovered
they were genuine Chanel
and worth a fair amount of money.
At this point I should say
that I straightaway telephoned
the Taxi Commission
to find out how to turn them in.
But I didn't.
Instead, I sold them on eBay.
My family chastised me
for my dubious morality.
The next day
I lost my far more costly fur hat in a taxi.
The irony eased my conscience,
and I had to smile.
For I had encountered
the greater,
the larger,
the cosmic
Lost and Found.

BLACKHEAD

I've never met anyone
who can resist the temptation
to squeeze a blackhead.
It doesn't even have to be
your own blackhead.
The ones on your boyfriend's back,
for example,
offer their own unique pleasure,
and the man who submits
is a sport indeed.
(You must reward him
by showing him the spoils.)
What is it about this tiny black dot
that so invites,
so demands our attention?
There it sits in its pore,
too secure, too smug.
We rise to the challenge.
Out with the evil intruder!
It may resist, but the harder it holds,
the more determined we fight,
and we will have it out at all costs,
even ugly red marks.
Finally it explodes forth.
Ah, gratification.
There is your trophy
on the tip of your finger.
You must examine it.
Admire its size.
Tell me, what else in life

[continued]

offers an opportunity
for such pure and simple
triumph?

NO PROBLEM

"No problem."
If any two words strike fear in my heart,
it's those.
I may be perfectly calm and coping.
Just seeking a little help.
But when I hear those two words,
my hair stands on end
and my instinct says, "flee."
When I have a problem,
give me someone with
questions and concerns.
Who sees everything that could
possibly go wrong.
Who acknowledges there may be
some rough spots along the way,
but then quietly assures me
he or she can handle it.
"No problem" has entered
our problem-filled lives
like a miracle cure,
infecting our daily vocabulary like a virus.
I can think of only one other phrase
that makes me this nervous:
"Don't worry."

GOAL!

Watching a soccer game is like
filming a television commercial.
If you've never been on a shoot,
here's what happens, basically:
nothing.
There is the illusion
of a great deal of activity.
Lots of scurrying about
that comes to naught.
You watch and watch and watch and
watch and watch and watch and watch.
Finally, your attention wanders.
BOOM!
In that instant
the one important thing,
the one essential thing,
the one thing that is
your whole reason for being there,
the one thing that you absolutely had to see,
well you know.
You missed it.

CUSTOMER SERVICE

As I prepare to make the call
to Customer Service,
I take a deep breath and remind myself
that losing my temper solves nothing.
I patiently listen to the series of choices
which we technology-weary consumers
have learned is called a "menu,"
and obediently make my selection,
thinking that now I will be connected
to the proper department.
"Please enter your account number now."
I obey.
"Please enter your telephone number now."
Once again, I obey.
"Please enter your zip code now."
Like a soldier, I obey.
This is really clever, I remember thinking
the first time it happened.
Now, when I finally get to speak
to a real live human being,
she'll already have all that information.
"Thank you,"
the recording informs me,
"you are being transferred to a
Customer Service Representative."
Pay dirt!
I have passed the test,
run the gauntlet,
filled all requirements.
I am rewarded

[continued]

with their most treasured resource,
the resource so precious,
they didn't want her to waste
her valuable time
asking me for routine information
a computer could handle.
And don't you know –
the first thing she asks me for
is my account number,
my telephone number,
and my zip code.
Do not bother to protest.
I can tell you from experience.
Logic loses.

STUPID

"I'm so stupid."
"Please help me out here."
"I can't believe I did such a dumb thing."
Although your therapist will tell you
not to engage in self-deprecation,
my experience in the busines world
teaches me the contrary.
It seems there is nothing so endearing,
so likely to elicit a helpful response,
than the unabashed admission
that you are an idiot —
or if not a total moron,
at least on a level of intelligence
far below that of the person
from whom you are seeking a favor.
So call yourself names.
Confess to shame.
Get what you want.
And privately
pat yourself on the back.

MISSA SOLEMNIS

We kept turning corners
as we chased the line's tail.
I was starting to feel like a teenager
waiting to get into a rock concert.
But these were older faces,
and there was a notable absence of police.
What event had drawn such a crowd?
None less than a free performance
by the New York Philharmonic
of a Missa Solemnis
to fill the grand spaces
of the Cathedral of Saint John the Divine.
How heavenly, indeed.
And the night, a summer's dream.
By the time we reached
the Cathedral's door,
the only place left to sit was the floor,
where we joined the legions
camped and cramped
in apses and naves miles from the stage.
No more!
From hereon in,
I'll take my music on CD.
Or the occasional splurge
for genuine, overpriced,
paid-for seats,
waiting just for he and me,
right up front or
forget it.

BANK THEFT

I'm feeling very clever indeed.
I figured out how to trick the ATM
into giving me more than $500 in one day
when I'm about to leave for a trip.
Gather round, I will share the scam.
Get your $500 limit,
but don't put your bankcard
back in your wallet –
you will need it very quickly.
As you pry your twenties loose
from the cash slot,
prepare your bankcard for the next hit.
If you do this fast enough,
you can go for another round of $500
before the first withdrawal
hits the computer.
Funny, you feel like a thief.
Like you're cheating or something.
Then the thought hits you.
Hey, this is my money.

FREE SAMPLES

The truck was parked illegally
at a busy curb in midtown
and two hired hands
in the back of the truck
were handing out samples of something
to passers-by who eagerly accepted.
This drew such attention,
those bright little boxes
were flying in every direction.
I stopped on my bicycle
to get me one.
A truck driver to my right asked
could I get him one.
It was "new microwave something"
and it wasn't until it was
tucked into my basket
that I discovered it was
"microwave extra crispy french fries."
Fat chance.
But I wasn't going to miss my chance.
Nor was anybody else.
What is the mystique of
a free sample of almost anything
that makes us clamor to get ours,
even makes us feel cheated if we don't?
We may work well and live well.
But if these free fries are any indication,
we're starving.

3. DAYLIGHT SAVINGS

DAYLIGHT SAVINGS

Tomorrow
morning will come a little early
as we spring into the season.
Some of us will be confused,
some of us will be late.
We will reset our clocks
and computers
and microwaves
and telephones
and VCR's
and answering machines.
I don't mind.
To me,
it's all about undoing damage,
returning to the rightful state of things.
Tonight
I go to bed with the reassurance
that indeed winter is only a phase,
and warmth will always follow.
I love this night.
I gladly forfeit the hour,
small sacrifice
to greater light.

The buds the buds
the newborn buds
are popping out
all over my tree
like bumps in the road
on the way to Spring.
Tomorrow we will have snow,
for that is the way of New York weather.
But I have seen the buds
and even though the snow
may give them one more huff and a fluff
I know that soon
I will renew my friendship
with the air and
there, for me,
is the beauty and hope
of the passing years.

MAGNOLIAS

In March no matter
how maddening the weather,
how confusing the signs,
the sleet and snow –
the magnolias know.
There have been smaller signals
sent out by lesser trees,
their buds giving unconvincing hints
of better days to come.
But today I have spotted
the lavender-ripening-into-purple
of a magnolia blossom.
I find these huge, soft, lavish
tree flowers
so miraculous
it makes a believer of me.
In this year of terror
in which all assumptions
are open to question,
I go home tonight assured
that at least one more time
there will
in fact
be spring.

PEACHES

I've been waiting for peaches.
Each day, I check the bins.
Apples.
Bananas.
Grapes, I hate grapes.
Today I spotted the first of them.
Peaches, beautiful peaches, I've missed you.
Spent $3.75 for two of them.
And it was worth every sweet bite.
You don't always find such perfect ones.
And usually not until
the full flush of summer.
Firm, but succulent.
That magic thing that happens
when the pulp hits your mouth.
Juices flow.
Nothing's as satisfying and virtuous
as a peach.
And no peach ever tastes as good
as the first good one of the season.

BICYCLE

Dodging danger
down the lanes of Ninth Avenue
I pedal with a pleasure
that's hard to explain
to those who know
I am hardly intrepid.
I am frightened by the subway
for gods sakes,
yet I'm somehow undaunted
by this traffic.
I have learned they are not all bad,
these roaring, rushing,
fast and furious four-wheeled
hurtling masses of metal.
They may resent my presence,
my fragile frame impeding their race
to the next red light,
but I have found to my amazement —
and my survival will affirm —
they'd really rather not hit me.
I don't claim to have never
been close to disaster.
But the pleasure of getting
from here to there
in the open air
on my own two wheels —
my iPod piping music into my ears —
is so profound,
the experience so exhilarating,
the triumph of movement and music

[continued]

over madness
so strong an affirmation of sanity
in my daily routine,
that fear is not a factor.
Or so I say.
Until one day
they come to wheel me away.

MUSIC

When I'm in a really foul mood,
I refuse to listen to music.
I particularly refuse to sing.
Or dance.
I'm no fool.
I know it will make me feel better.
And right then,
I want to feel lousy.
Music messes all that up.
Throws your anger all off balance.
Sneaks up on your stubborn spitefulness.
Seduces you out of your sulk.
Sucks the self pity right out of you.
So if you're feeling
like the whole world stinks
and you want to keep it that way,
get yourself into a corner
that's far away from music.
Given even the slightest opening,
music will completely ruin your rotten day.

SAXOPHONE

There's a guy in Central Park
getting an unbelievable sound
out of a saxophone.
This isn't even so uncommon.
He's alone on a bench.
And nobody is paying any attention.
This is New York.
We're cool.
The tune is autumn leaves
but summer is hot upon us.
The sweet notes have no sour neighbors
to complain through the walls of
the building where he lives.
Is he performing?
Practicing?
Are these sounds for us,
or simple self expression?
Who cares?
As I bike by,
I give him the slightest hint of a wave
and he acknowledges with
the barest hint of a nod.

BLUE JAY

I'm such a city kid,
I was thrilled to see a blue jay
perch on the porch
outside the kitchen window.
I was visiting my brother in San Mateo,
where people have decks,
and there are birds beyond
pigeons and sparrows.
That afternoon,
we hung a bird feeder
and waited expectantly
behind the big window.
Within minutes, the first jay arrived.
He darted and danced,
checking it out from all angles.
Soon he was lord of the manor,
feeding every two minutes,
and we joked about how
he'd soon be too fat to fly.
Wait, what's this?
We trembled with excitement —
here come more birds,
other kinds,
little ones.
But the jay would have no part of it.
He zoomed, he flapped his wings,
he even beat his beak
on the wooden railing
to chase them away.
In the next days, we saw nothing but jays.

[continued]

I was no longer impressed
by the brilliance of their feathers.
I felt truly sad as I departed
for the daily birdplay of New York life.
But today there is good news
from California.
The jays have relented
and the small birds have begun
to share in the bounty.
I am once again reminded
that some things just take time.

GERANIUMS

The blossoms on my geraniums
are taking turns.
Like little leap-flowers.
Just as one of them fully matures,
the next one starts opening.
As the first starts to wither,
the second comes into full flower,
and a third one begins to open.
There's a whole cluster of tight little buds
just waiting their turn.
As if my windowsill
were the most desirable place on earth
and everyone's just lining up
for their moment in the sun.

BIRD CALLS

I don't speak bird
but I often listen to their calls
and wonder what they are saying.
My nephew and I are sharing this
because he tells me that yesterday
he hung his new birdfeeder,
and though he hears the birds in the sky,
they are just flying by,
ignoring his tasty seeds
and his hungry eyes.
I tell him he can only sit and wait,
for he can't hang a sign
or send out dinner invitations.
We must trust that birds
have a way of their own,
and they'll discover his offerings
in their own bird time.
It's not such an odd idea.
After all,
we don't go running
the very next day
just because
there's a new
restaurant in town.

THREE SEASONS

One day last winter
a plastic bag
was swirled from the sidewalk
and snagged on a tree.
It's been flapping there ever since
and no act of nature will take it away.
If it were a kite,
I could romanticize its presence,
imagining the small tragedy
of a child losing his airborne toy.
But this unsightly intruder —
stamped with the colors of
the local Duane-Reade —
leaves me indignant.
It's the way I feel at the beach
when my eyes,
expecting shells,
encounter condoms.
Each day I look out my window,
hoping the tree has shaken it loose.
Or perhaps a bird has plucked it away.
Spring arrives.
Buds emerge and blossom.
Limp and faded, the bag hangs on.
Blossoms fall.
Green foliage grows lush and strong.
But though its leaves almost hide it,
the tree still suffers its tenacious tenant.
Now it's August,
and we're coming full circle.
Will it fall?

DEER

In the awesome heat of a Texas day,
we ride our bikes along a country road,
stopping for snapshots
and sips of water.
Shhh. . .
a sighting.
We are so excited —
we who grew up with cars and
no green fields,
no high grass or leafy brush.
A deer.
She is so close.
We freeze —
we are even more still than she,
afraid to make her flee.
We stare,
and she returns our gaze
across the total quiet of the moment.
Here come more:
one, two, now there are six,
crossing quick and calm,
trespassing through someone's front yard,
pausing to nibble at shrubs,
disappearing finally
(releasing us to resume our ride)
into the trees.
How our concrete lives
are so moved
by such a small spectacle.

DOGGIE

Child meets dog:
an encounter at knee level.
I watch the child in the stroller
as it approaches the dog.
Fascination fixes on his face.
A strong invisible force
seems to pull the stroller towards the dog,
and the mother follows.
"Doggie, doggie!"
The mother stops
and descends to the drama.
"Nice dog."
It's OK, the dog seems to say,
you can pet me,
I'm a sturdy fellow.
Small arms reach out with
palms open,
flailing at the fur,
and usually end up hitting the dog.
Child squeals with delight.
Dog sighs.
A good deed done.

SPRING SNOW

In the startlingly beautiful weeks of April,
the bare brown trees
take turns producing blossoms,
some white,
some pink,
some outrageously fuschia.
These are delicate blooms,
meant only to birth the green that follows,
and easily loosened
with the slightest breeze.
The paths in the park
are strewn with their petals.
As I pass beneath the trees
on a windy day,
I savor the gentle storm,
the benign blizzard
of spring snow.

UPSTAIRS DOWNSTAIRS

Having lived in an apartment all my life,
I can't get the hang of a two-story house.
It's a given that
whatever I want downstairs,
I've left upstairs.
And no matter how hard I try
to remember to bring it with me
to whatever level,
there's always something I forget.
I think they built two-story houses
as modern living's answer
to our sedentary lives.
For it guarantees at least
a small bit of exertion
without going to a gym.
People who live in two story houses
have developed various techniques
to deal with the problem.
They routinely leave their
downstairs belongings
at the foot of the stairs
to either be remembered
or stumbled over.
Similarly, objects are stacked
at the top of the stairs
for the next trip down.
But the double-decker dweller
soon learns not to notice
and the trick quickly loses its effect.
As I sit here upstairs writing,

[continued]

I suddenly remember a call I need to make.
But of course I've left my address book
in the handbag
I so cleverly left downstairs
near the front door
so I wouldn't have to make
a last minute climb
as I'm about to leave the house.
What to do?
Look out the window
and enjoy the view.

KIDS

Kids don't watch where they're going.
Kids careen.
As if the whole world
will get out of their way.
Completely oblivious.
Inconsiderate little things.
Hog the sidewalk
as they skip along three-abreast.
Pour onto the pavement in packs
as they emerge from school.
Kids change direction without signaling.
Veer off course on a whim.
Defy all attempts to get around them.
Kids on bicycles are particularly dangerous.
Swerve.
Sway.
Fall down.
Does it ever occur to kids
that another body might cross their path?
Don't they know
there are other folks on the street?
Don't they know
they should always look in both directions?
Or check behind them
as they walk backwards?
No, I guess they don't know.
At least not yet.
I guess that's what
being a kid is about.

LUCY

The front door opened and Lucy shot in
with explosive force.
She seemed to run into all of the rooms
at the same time.
Then she bounded up the stairs,
whizzed through those spaces,
and flew back down to where
Claudia was still taking off her coat
and kissing us hello.
Now she directed her energy at us,
sniffing,
dashing back and forth,
and we returned her wags with smiles.
The whole house seemed
touched by her presence.
We sat down for conversation
and Lucy curled at Claudia's feet,
but her eyes were on the lookout,
her ears cocked at every sound.
"Come here, girl, come on,"
I urged from my seat.
She paused,
then she came to me,
and I felt blessed with affection.
Such is the power of
doggie love.

SUMMER

The last day of July.
I like to eat my summer slowly
like a piece of chocolate cake.
Memorial Day is
an enormous mound
of anticipated pleasure on my plate.
I savor the days like mouthfuls,
the warmth melting the hurts in my heart.
I watch with dismay
as the Fourth of July
is too quickly the first of August,
and suddenly it's Labor Day.
How soon the summer slips away.
But hey,
what's this melancholy musing?
It's the last day of July
with the promise of heat and no rain.
What's to complain?
Many more days before goodybye.
There, I've cured myself.
Or at least,
almost convinced myself.

98.6 degrees.
That's normal, right?
As right as 5,280 feet in a mile,
50 states,
and 8 slices in a large pizza.
Then why am I so amused?
Because we're in the middle
of a heat wave,
and everyone's wilting
while I —
who suffer all winter
while others romp with ruddy cheeks —
am feeling like
everything's right with the world.
I just checked the thermometer
and it's exactly
98.6 degrees.
Outside.

WHEELS

Everything has wheels
in Central Park on Saturday 85°.
Bicycles.
Rollerblades.
Skateboards.
The pretzel man
and the soda man next to him.
A wheelchair,
one with a motor, one without.
A shopping cart
filled with baseball bats and balls.
A helicopter.
Those big grey trash bins have wheels too.
So does the cart behind the horse.
Dogs don't.
Babies have lots of wheels.
On their strollers.
Carriages.
There's a small baby cart
hitched to the back of mom's bicycle.
I think maybe even
the Metropolitan Museum has wheels
but they don't use them very often.

HEAT

In Florida in August,
you walk out the door of your
air-conditioned room
and the heat wafts up to meet you
like a huge marshmallow.
To me,
it feels like a welcoming committee,
all smiling and happy to see me,
and I respond.
Even the stubbornest negativity
about life, love, lunch
or nothing in particular
melts into the arms of this mystical power.
My skin softens.
My body is light and I feel,
yes, graceful.
A state of grace, a state of graceful.
And I am grateful.
I have sworn I will not spend
one more winter in the north,
and perhaps this year I will find a way.
This is not just about temperature.
This is about feeling wanted.

NO AIR CONDITIONING

On hot days
I sometimes deliberately
don't turn on the air conditioner.
I open the windows –
through which no air enters
because my apartment has
no cross ventilation –
and I experience
the stillness of summer air.
The slightly moist sponge
of New York humidity
touches my arms and face.
I try to do things slowly
and calmly.
I listen to the heat-muffled sounds
of trucks and buses passing below.
Everything has a padded quality.
The best part
is knowing that it's summer,
which I sadly forget
when I close the windows
and refrigerate my living quarters.
The heat invites me out,
out of my walls and tables
and typing,
out into the street.
Perhaps I'll go buy a piece of fruit
from the cart on the corner.
Or descend with no more purpose
than mailing a letter.

[continued]

I don't need to stop to
put on a coat.
I thrive on this freedom,
this easy connection with the street,
where even in New York City
I can catch a glimpse of sky.

EARLY SNOW

The snow swept into the city
too soon this year —
even before the last leaves
had their chance to fall.
I watch from the warmth of my window
as the fragile flakes
are propelled by the wind
in an angular dive.
I look down as mounds form
on the tops of parked cars.
In the street,
the slow moving traffic
is grinding white fluff
into grey mush.
Even through my closed windows
I hear the sloshing sounds of
spinning wheels
punctuated with scraping of
shovels on pavements.
I find myself hating
this falling phenomenon
that inhibits movement
and sends winter warnings
across my TV screen.
I try to remember the beauty of snow,
the graceful arcs created by drifts,
vast white plains
so bright they hurt the eyes.
Snow is for people who live in the country,
for children on sleds,

[continued]

for folks on skis. . .
but not for me.
Not until they figure out a way
to make snow fall on a hot sunny day.

4. COLOR CODING

COLOR CODING

Have you seen the color-coded kids
in the park?
This is inner city summer in New York.
Clusters of kids
from community centers
are herded by their counselors
to their activities —
a playground,
a ball field,
a public pool,
an outing to the museum —
wearing bright little tee-shirts that
go down to their knees,
the names of their day camps
across their small chests.
Each cluster has a different color —
here a group in sunbright red,
now a group in lime green,
another in fiery yellow.
This color-coding,
most likely born out of the need to
distinguish one group from another,
also seems to have the effect
of creating a sense of belonging,
and I wonder if the kids feel
the strength of that.
On my way through the park,
I encounter the little caravans.
As they pass,
holding hands,

[continued]

or bouncing along in a loose parade,
the rebel individual in me
plays an impish trick.
I find myself thinking
I'd like to be color-coded too.
I'd like to know where I belong.

CIGARS

Everyone should smoke cigars.
Consider the virtues.
You look very important.
You command attention.
Everyone can smell you.
Inhale you.
Absorb you.
Experience your emanations.
In lungs.
Blood.
The very core of their being.
Your kiss has a distinctive flavor.
Your fingers take on the patina
of well-worn nicotine.
Your aroma lingers on clothes.
Hair.
Skin.
You are undeniable.
Unforgettable.
Unbearable.

TONGUE

I looked with jaded eyes
past her hair dyed the color of
maraschino cherries.
It was the mouth that made me look again,
as I caught a glimpse of a
flashing silver ball
on the tip of her tongue.
She kept flicking it,
rubbing it against her lips,
poking it,
sucking on it.
A pierced tongue.
I felt it as much as I saw it.
A sharp metal stake
driven through my own tongue.
Driven painfully
through tender, sensitive flesh.
An irritating metal ball
always present in my mouth.
I wanted to spit it out,
repel it,
be free of it.
Yet there she was across from me,
undoubtedly feeling very
cool.

NAILS

In the nail salon on Friday,
I join in the ritual.
For an hour or more,
I allow my hands to be
taken out of commission.
This is not a nice feeling.
I can't write or read
(although some more advanced women
have mastered this).
I can't fiddle with my computer.
I can't make phone calls.
I can't make myself a cup of coffee,
or fuss with papers,
or do any of the things
that normally occupy my mind and time.
Damn, I can't even scratch my nose.
In desperation,
I find myself engaging in conversation
with a fellow victim at the next table
about the relative merits
of gel versus glue manicures.
I hate this.
But all my life I have looked in awe
at women who could have ten long nails
at the same time.
Who could polish them
and not have chips by the next day.
My hands seem to have been made
for other things,
and I comforted myself with that.

[continued]

I'd rather play the piano.
Or make pottery.
Or play tennis.
Even pry loose a staple with abandon.
But spread the news, sisters!
Today, through the miracle
of modern science and acrylics,
we can all have long beautiful nails!
I never thought I'd see the day when
I'd be one of those women
on a Friday afternoon.
But then, I never thought I'd see the day
when someone would look at me and say,
"Nice nails!"

FUCK YOU

How did such a sensual act
become so tinged with anger?
Why is "fuck you" an expression of rage
instead of a promise of pleasure?
Does the beast within us
respond to the sound,
of that harsh strident "k"
as in prick, or smack,
or strike someone back?
Or is it something more insidious,
some cultural virus that
infects our vocabulary
and turns sex slang
into mud sling.
Our everyday speech is sprinkled with fuck
like cement filling in the space between tiles.
The fuckin' doctor kept me waiting an hour.
The fuckin' operator put me on hold.
The fuckin' microwave isn't fuckin' working.
And who gives a fuck, anyway?
Fucking may not always be making love,
but need it be a dirty word?
I am a sensual, sexual human being.
Fuck me.

FALL

I'm sitting in the car
beside my country friend
in awe and fascination.
The yellow leaves reflect the sun
creating light even as day dims.
We drive.
One tall tree is a crimson slash
among a shorter cluster
of rust and tan.
Suddenly a blaze of red
so intense at the side of the road,
we pause a moment
to pay homage to its splendor.
What perverse force
created this spectacle
so rich and lush,
so full of color,
to signal the coming
of cold and grey?
Fall is too beautiful
to be about dying
but it is.

I've never been so aware of trees
as I am this spring.
They mark the changing of the season
like public pronouncements.
For the last few weeks,
I've watched in fascination
as they've slowly transformed themselves
out of their winter invisibility.
The first indication
was the appearance of bumps,
silly little protrusions,
almost imperceptible,
but distinctly swelling at regular intervals
along each bare branch.
The bumps soon began to open,
revealing hints of color —
sometimes white, sometimes pink,
sometimes an improbable orange
that made me think of rust.
As the days passed,
flowers began poking out,
not all at once,
but in a staggered sequence
surely orchestrated by some great gardener.
First was the week of the
white-flower trees,
displaying copious clusters of tiny petals.
Then the pink trees took their cue.
Next, the magnolias on center stage.
As new trees performed,

[continued]

the earlier players
had their petals pushed out by
bright green, burgeoning foliage.
Today the streets are strewn with
fallen white flowers,
and it reminds me of autumn
only so much prettier
because it's about beginnings, not endings.
Why are the trees catching my eye
so very much this year?
I think I'm looking for life signs,
needing to be inspired to grow,
to find my own flowers,
to come into my own kind of green.

BAD GIRL

I've been reprimanded.
I had been parking my bicycle
in the hallway outside my apartment,
and the management of my co-op
sent me a letter.
This must be serious.
A written, official, on-the-record record
of my bad behavior.
I can't resort to my usual indignation,
because I know damn well
I was breaking the rules.
I walked around all day
with this awful feeling.
The kind of feeling that clings to you
when you wake up after a dream
in which you've been shamed or humiliated.
Perhaps I can make an extra effort
to be kind and friendly.
Smile and chat with a neighbor in the lobby.
There, I feel a little better.
Clean up the kitchen.
Do someone a favor, that always helps.
How can I restore myself to
a state of grace?
Why can't I be one of those
upstanding citizens who never tries to
get away with anything?
Why can't I go home after school and
do my homework so I can
walk into the classroom tomorrow

[continued]

with a smile on my face
and peace in my heart?
Our Father who art in heaven,
forgive me my sins.
Please tell me I'm not a bad girl.

PARTICIPATION

In desperation,
after torturous hours
struggling to stay awake
during deadly boring meetings,
I decided to try a new strategy.
Participation.
Instead of sitting there
"keeping a low profile" as they like to say
in play-it-safe business lingo,
I started to speak up.
Take chances.
I found my own comments
far more interesting
than anything else I was hearing.
The mere act of talking —
even if I wasn't saying anything
particularly brilliant —
kept me awake.
I gradually grew more daring.
Questioned the unintelligible.
Challenged orthodoxy.
Allowed my sense of humor.
Teased people.
Complimented someone
when I heard a good idea.
Meetings became more tolerable.
Even occasionally stimulating.
Other people responded.
Brains kicked in.
Personalities emerged.

[continued]

What had started out
as a reckless act
born of desperation,
had turned into a quality
I had never thought to aspire to.
Leadership.

NANNIES

It's mid-morning
on the streets of the Upper West
or Upper East
or wherever the upper middle class
calls home.
The nannies are out in force
with their strollers.
Black nannies.
White babies.
As always, I'm conflicted.
I rebel at the phenomenon of history
and economics
and racism
that leaves black babies at home
while their mothers tend white babies
to be able to feed their own.
I admire the goodness and decency
that allows these surrogate mothers
to nurture their charges with tenderness.
As I watch a nanny caress the cheek
of a silken-haired cherub,
I remember that these are babies.
They are innocent.
And these women are
good enough
and wise enough
to know that.

COFFEE

I've been walking for 3 blocks already,
and there's no Starbucks in sight.
I want a cup of coffee.
It used to be so simple.
Any old deli would do.
Today I realize that
I too have become a victim of the
designer coffee phenomenon.
I don't feel right anymore
buying my coffee in a store that sells
cheese danish and cigarettes.
I'm not a coffee connoisseur.
Yet here I am
going out of my way
for the privilege of paying
triple the price.
And I get to stand in line.
I'm horrified.
Not by them.
By me.
Where are my defenses?
My counterattack?
I'm going home to make
my own pot of coffee.
Trouble is,
I bought the beans at Starbucks.

SPONSORSHIP

The soccer field is
surrounded by corporate logos,
those familiar giants of
prime-time athletic patronage.
Today the women's teams
are fighting for the World Cup,
and America is watching.
In the upper left hand corner
of the television screen
we can regularly check
the time remaining and the score,
and here, too,
they have not missed a chance
for advertising revenue.
The ESPN logo is fixed,
but at right,
the place of honor rotates.
Gatorade. . .
Bud Light. . .
Adidas. . .
Monistat.
Monistat? Time out!
Is today's score really brought to us
by a cure for vaginal yeast infections?
Something feels wrong.
I don't like seeing my private parts
hung up on a scoreboard
just because the players are women.
It makes me feel
we're not an audience,

[continued]

we're not athletes,
we're not people.
To an advertiser,
we're just millions of captive vaginas.

BREASTS

Breasts loom larger than ever
since the advent of
silicone, seamless bras
and lowcut lycra.
On television, in the movies,
and everywhere I go,
women wear their bulging breasts
as if they were oblivious
to the sexual nature
of this part of their anatomy.
Small breasts like mine are guilty too,
but big ones must surely be harder to ignore.
I wonder how any man
can keep a straight face,
can fail to react,
in the face of this phenomenon.
"Hello," she says
to the salesman in the store
from behind her D-cupped chest,
"do you carry . . ."
(does he hear the rest?)
I can't imagine chatting with —
and pretending not to notice —
a man whose penile prowess
were protruding,
its outlines clearly visible,
from within tight lycra pants.
I'm a woman and I don't get it.
And we wonder why so many men
are confused.

DOG BOUQUET

In New York City,
dogs get walked in bunches.
The resulting arrangements
are mobile displays.
Consider the aesthetic possibilities.
Size.
Shape.
Color.
Texture.
There's so much to work with.
The leashes are the stems.
Each has its own unique blossom.
Here for example,
a curly white poodle
tucks nicely under the chin
of a sleek golden retriever.
The shadings and folds of a pudgy boxer
make perfect contrast
to the long legs and taut body
of a grey weimaraner.
Now a low-lying
copper-colored dachshund.
And one really tall head
to top the arrangement:
The dog walker.

PERFUME

Walking into Bloomingdale's,
you will be attacked.
Be prepared to walk the gauntlet,
as they close in from both sides
smiling and pointing their sprays.
The pretty girls in shiny lips.
The pretty boys all super-groomed.
Do not succumb.
Do not fall into "Temptation."
Do not drink the "Poison."
Because in the past few years,
the true talents in the fragrance industry
have all been at work in
the naming department —
and they've let the gremlins take over
the smelling department.
There are foul brews that
make you want to gag.
Perfumes that reek like old plastic.
Cloying scents that
cause your nasal passages to shrivel.
Men think it's sexy
to smell like stale tobacco.
Young women are crazy for
something that reminds me of mildew.
Once in Bloomingdale's,
curiosity got the better of me
and "Passion" overcame me.
I let them spray.
For the rest of the day,
I couldn't stand to be near me.

MANICURE

"I had a pedicure in Paris"
said the man
yes the man
sitting next to me in the nail salon
having a man
icure
and chatting with the man
icurist who was filing away.
I have been noticing this phenomen-
on lately.
They used to be such an oddity
in this bastion of beauty.
But lately they enter with regularity,
and take their place beside us,
we high-maintenance members
of our species,
putting their hands on the table
with temerity.
And why not?
I like a man with a well-tended hand,
fingers strong and firm,
nails clipped short and clean.
Although even in my enlightened state
I would draw the line
at polish that goes beyond clear
and ventures into colors
we women hold dear,
like "Ballet Slippers"
and "Wicked."

WOMEN'S

Let's fight.
Let's strike.
Let's write to Congress.
Let's resurrect the feminist movement
(that's not a bad idea anyway).
It's about time somebody did something.
Think about it.
Every time you go to the movies.
The theater.
A concert.
A restaurant.
Is it discrimination?
Disdain?
Simple stupidity?
Any moron could figure out
that when it comes to
going to the bathroom
it takes a woman longer to do her thing
than it takes a man to undo his.
So get on it, you guys who allocate space.
It's only fair.
It's only right.
Stop stalling.
We need more stalls!

TRANSFORMATION

How old are these girls
sitting across from me
Saturday night on the subway
from Queens to Manhattan?
As we begin our journey,
they look about twelve.
Plain.
Pale.
Rather drab.
But they are excited.
Each has a bulging cosmetic bag on her lap,
and is holding a small mirror in one hand.
I watch, pretending not to, as they apply:
Foundation.
Eyebrows.
Shadow.
Eyelash curler.
Mascara.
Blusher.
And finally, lipstick.
The transformation is astounding.
The same faces are now glowing,
not just with makeup,
but with self-awareness.
They know they are beautiful.
As they get up
and wait for the doors to open,
men's eyes are upon them.
We have reached Manhattan.
They have reached maturity.

HOUSEWARMING

My geraniums are growing.
I never would have bought myself a plant —
they're a pain in the neck
and they always die.
But my aunt and uncle
brought me these two living things.
Housewarming presents.
One with bright red flowers
that go very well with my color scheme.
In fact, that one actually won me over.
The other had fuchsia flowers
which oddly offended me.
No problem, since within two days
the flowers had all fallen off.
Leaves shriveled and turned yellow.
It was just a matter of how long to wait
before I could throw them out
in good conscience.
(I am fond of my aunt and uncle.)
So I kept my little houseguests
longer than I might have.
Even gave them water
when it occurred to me.
Wouldn't you know
the spunky little things recovered?
Bright green crinkly leaves
sprouted out of the stems.
New ones every day.
Growing so fast,
I could see the difference in hours.

[continued]

But three days ago, I became really hooked.
Ohmygosh, those aren't just green things.
They're buds.
Flower buds.
I'm going to have a flower.
But nature will have the last laugh.
It's the fuchsia one
that's putting forth the flowers.

ENGLISH ACCENT

Why are English accents
so intimidating?
The sound of those clipped,
perfectly formed words,
those elegant vowels,
immediately puts distance
between me and the speaker.
No matter how hard I try to hold my own,
I feel sloppy, unkempt —
as if the other person
were wearing a well-tailored suit
and I've been caught in my sweats.
But though I cringe at the sound
of a bad New York accent,
there's something I love
about the way we communicate.
Open.
Informal.
Spontaneous.
I think it's easier to laugh
when your lips aren't so stiff.
So I'll take Manhattan,
the Bronx and Long-guy-land.
And God save the Queen!

SNOW

There are these big white things
floating past my window.
Lots of them.
They're so funny-looking,
it's hard to believe they're natural.
I think maybe my street
is actually the floor of
one of those glass spheres
you buy in the tourist stores
which you turn upside down and shake
and oversized flakes
fall in a frenzy
until they've all landed
and everything
settles
down.

COUSIN KENNY

My cousin Kenny
needs to know
why things work.
I, on the other hand,
am grateful not to know
why my computer crashed
and how to jam a RAM
into the designated slot.
It's not that I'm stupid.
It's that Kenny has a knack,
an instinctive way of
untangling certain problems,
an amazing ability
to locate the core of the cause,
a stubborn streak
that fuels the flame
of his ferocious desire
to conquer the mysteries
of technology.
I watch with wonder
and without a bit of envy.
I know there are things that stymie him
that I can take on without batting an eye.
We are a good team:
He being he.
Me being me.

MEN COOKING

My father never cooked anything
besides the cane he boiled
to craft into his bassoon reeds.
I can't even recall him frying an egg.
And so I am amazed at the number of men
I encounter these days
who love, or say they love, to cook.
Yes, I had my days in the kitchen
discovering the joys of cooking
but I've long since grown bored
with the shopping and chopping,
the fuss and the muss,
all to concoct a creation
enjoyed so briefly
and then gone forever,
like a sand castle swept away by the tide.
These days I've turned
my creative endeavors
to forms more enduring:
a poem or a song,
something to save and savor at will.
But please don't take offense,
you men who love to cook.
I say if you love it,
go at it with the zest
once reserved for success
in the corporate world.
In fact, dear man,
I've had a long day.
Is dinner ready yet?

CIGARETTES

She knows she shouldn't smoke them.
But like my father who died from them,
she simply can't stop.
Having been a smoker myself,
I'm extremely understanding –
perhaps too understanding.
What makes me crazy
is the way she collects those coupons
that come on each pack.
They're like frequent smoker points.
In fact, each coupon says "5 miles."
That's 5 miles closer
to lung cancer and heart disease.
She piles them up so she can be rewarded
with a big red Marlboro sportsbag.
We are such goddamn victims,
gratified beyond all reason
when we get something for free.
To me that big red sportsbag
is like carrying around a sign that says,
"I polluted my lungs with
300 packs of cigarettes
to get this for free.
Aren't I cool?"
No, sweet sister, you are not cool.
You've been had.
You want something for free?
Let me give you a hug for
putting down those
dirty smelly
killer cigarettes.

CREATION

Someone is crafting a chandelier,
a display of splendor
on a grand scale.
Hundreds of delicate,
intricate components
are being formed in varying stages,
perched in their places
in perfect balance
without the boredom of symmetry.
Each is an exhibit
in soft lavenders and purples.
It's all unfolding before my eyes
with no workman in sight.
I stand in awe before the spectacle.
I am witnessing
the blossoming of a
magnolia tree.

SUN WORSHIP

Sandra lives for the sun.
Her latin complexion sops it up
and sautés to a golden brown
like onions in a pan.
Sandra knows there is power in this color,
starkly dramatic
with her short black hair,
sleekly seductive
on her carefully tended body.
But the seductress is also the victim,
seduced by the power,
a slave to its call.
She makes pilgrimages to her black tar roof,
treks to beaches or poolsides
not occasionally, but obsessively.
She convinces herself
she will somehow be spared
from the rays' aging ways,
their cancerous implications.
That her after-beach balms
can undo the harm.
As I watch her turn
from winter white to burnished bronze,
I squelch my green envy.
I think of my own various obsessions,
past and present,
my own sacrifices to the gods of beauty.
I look at Sandra's gloriously golden face
and force myself to also look beyond it,
to remember reason.

[continued]

And anyway,
I never did like
sweltering on the beach.

SIXTY DEGREES

In September,
when the living's been easy for months
and my arms have almost forgotten
the feel of long sleeves,
I suddenly realize that
each day is not just getting a little shorter,
but a little cooler.
80's. . .mid 70's. . .
my sweet hot summer is slipping away.
In this mood,
I greet with resentment
the first damn day
that descends into the sixties.
I do not welcome the warning
that winter is waiting.
That things like snow and gloves
will soon spoil the party.
No, sixty degrees is not balmy.
Not gentle.
Not nice in any way.
But that's
in September,
when the living's been easy.
Now it's February
and we've been too long
deep in the freeze,
resigned to heavy coats and
chapped lips and runny eyes and
hats,
oh hateful hats.

[continued]

In this mood,
I greet the arrival of sixty degrees
not with dismay
but appreciation.
Sixty is an invitation,
a reprieve,
a caress.
I open my coat, my body relaxes,
I actually smile.
Odd, I think,
this is the same sixty degrees
that felt so cold in September.

BACK TROUBLE

When your back has problems,
everyone's a doctor.
This part of the body seems to invite
the best intentions
and the greatest contention.
Though your doctor
has prescribed physical therapy,
your Aunt Joan
(who suffered the same problem)
counsels that
only chiropractic will cure you.
She's just about converted you,
when your friend Eddie
makes a convincing case for yoga.
Your boyfriend's co-worker
says his doctor ordered total bed rest.
Another well-wisher tells you
you're wasting your time and money
with traditional medicine,
when acupuncture can do it all.
The guy who fixes your computer
shares his saga,
wherein he tries everything
only to end up on the surgeon's table.
You are no longer your usual
disbelieving self,
for your pain has drilled holes
in your skepticism,
and your mind is fuzzy
from sleepless nights

[continued]

and a shelf full of pills.
Who to believe?
I don't know.
I do know that whatever
turns out to be the answer for me,
someday in the future
I, too,
am very likely to be
swearing by it.

5. SHARING JEWLERY

SHARING JEWELRY

As little girls we loved to rummage
in the jewelry boxes of our
mothers and grandmothers.
It was a form of play,
to pass the time
while adults sat in the other room
in endless conversation.
I remember the fascination with
those earrings and bracelets.
Now here we are,
years later,
sitting all together on a big bed
while conversation continues
in another room.
Gail has died,
and we her female family
by blood and marriage,
are sorting through
her lifetime collection of jewelry.
We have done our crying and trying
to imagine life without her.
We have stepped into that strange place
where it is acceptable to
look through her clothes,
opening drawers, selecting items,
fending off twinges of conditioned response
that we are violating her privacy.
Thus far we've done this separately.
But the jewelry we do together,
an intimacy of women,

[continued]

a communal rummaging,
nobody coveting.
Rather we are exchanging words like,
"Do you want those?"
"That one looks really good on you."
"I can't remember her wearing those."
"We bought those at a crafts fair."
"She liked those so much."
"How do these look on me?"
"No, no, if you want them, you take them."
There is surprising solace in our sisterhood.
Nothing feels bad here.
Gail is with us, and I almost hear her say,
"Yes, this is okay, I wanted it this way."

At the remembrance event,
I wear one beautiful piece
I have chosen for me,
knowing that each time I wear it,
I will treasure her.

LESSON

My grandmother taught me how to knit.
Between the stitches,
she taught me something more important.
She said if you're
almost finished knitting something
and you discover you made a mistake —
even back at the very beginning —
here's what you do.
You undo
everything
right back to where
you made the mistake.
She said if you don't,
it will always bother you.
And you will never be
happy and proud of your finished work.
I have on many occasions
tried to rationalize not going back
to undo a difficult labor.
In those moments,
my grandmother speaks to me.
I take a deep breath
and start unraveling,
as quickly as possible,
the wrongly wrought work.
When the mistake is undone,
I breathe a sigh of relief,
for the undoing is done,
and from here on,
I am building
instead of regretting.

BELLY

Portrait in pot belly and baseball cap.
This guy is every guy you've ever seen
who's drunk a little too much beer,
eaten a few too many slices,
lived a few too many years since
he's been to the ballfield
or cared.
His orange tee-shirt
stretches over the balloon
that begins just below his breast,
curving in front of him,
rounding the equator
at the belt of his jeans,
sloping back into hidden parts
that hopefully are in better shape
than his belly.
He's a good guy.
A good looking guy.
Probably going home to watch TV
with a good loving woman
who doesn't notice his belly
or care.

PHONE NUMBER

I still remember my phone number
from when I was a little girl.
(Do you?)
It occurs to me that
I probably never called that number,
since I was too young,
yet it has stayed with me
through all these years.
Did I learn it just from
listening to my mother
as she gave it to other people?
Or was I told to memorize it
in case I ever got lost
and had to ask an adult
to return me?
However it happened,
that number lives inside me
with a rhythm and a melody
as distinctive as a song.
Hit it, boys:
Hav-a-meyer six,
nine one two three.

BRANCHES

It's spring and the man is walking
with the long brown branches
tucked under his arm,
their ends wrapped in florist's paper.
At random intervals along the branches
are just-born blossoms,
soft spots of bright pink,
and I imagine the lovely effect
they will have in his living room.
But something feels wrong and
I rebel at the sight.
Those blossoms
haven't even had a chance.
Still in formation,
not quite in flower,
they've been hacked off
in their infancy.
I look again at the branches,
their back ends poking out of the paper
revealing the slashes
that tore them from their tree.
Let them be – don't you see?
It's spring.
This is a gentle thing.

PIANO

They took away my mother's piano.
It wasn't poverty that caused her to sell it.
It was old age.
Her fingers don't obey any more.
She tells me this matter-of-factly.
I wince with pain.
She tells me with just a hint of nostalgia
how her parents gave her that piano
when she was a girl.
Says she can't remember a time
when she didn't play the piano.
When she married,
that piano became
a member of her new household.
It was a baby grand,
but there was nothing baby about it.
It was an imposing piece of furniture,
walnut wood shining,
gracefully curved and commanding
the living room decor.
As a little girl,
I remember sneaking peeks
as my mother gave lessons.
I could hardly wait to be old enough
to take lessons myself.
When mom sat down to play,
she was transformed into an artist,
moving her hands in waving arcs,
as if coaxing the lyricism out of the keys.
My own lessons were in time abandoned,

[continued]

but the piano was always there,
welcoming me whenever
I'd be moved to return to it.
We all loved that piano.
But I know my mother loved it more.
It was a testament to her musicality,
her accomplishment,
an unbroken thread in her life.
Today she can no longer play,
and they've come to take it away.
She seems to have found a way
to make her peace with this.
I have not.

LUNCH WITH LILY

Lily is in trouble.
When she told me that,
I found it hard to believe.
Lily manages everything with
logic and laughter.
Lily is sweet.
Lily never forgets your birthday.
Lily has a husband.
Three children.
A pet.
A house.
A car.
Patience.
And she's so nice,
I don't even hate her for it.
Now she says she needs a friend.
Not the dozens of neighborhood friends
who have organized a community effort
to bring hot meals to her home every night.
Not the other contingent
which has organized a carpool
to help take her kids
to their various activities.
Lily says she needs a friend
with whom she can share how she feels.
Frightened.
Overwhelmed.
Tearful.
Out of control.
Lily's husband has been struck

[continued]

by a rampant form of leukemia
that puts him in daily danger of dying.
And she's asked me to have lunch.

THE MEN

There were so many husbands,
so many fathers
those summers we spent in the Catskills.
They arrived each Friday like immigrants
setting foot on our green country.
We, the kids and our mothers,
would stay all summer
to escape the heat and concrete
while the men went back each Monday
and sweated to sustain us.
In the mornings we put on our shorts,
went to day camp, swam in the creek,
chose up sides for baseball,
grew radishes and cucumbers,
wove lanyards and crafted clay pots.
At night we played ping-pong
in the barn we called the casino.
But on Friday night . . .
There were so many husbands,
so many fathers
those weekends in the Catskills.
They'd arrive in their cars,
and the bungalows buzzed
with a communal energy.
The men, the men.
Mothers became wives.
The casino became the center
for their social lives.
Folk dancing, lectures, raffles and theatre.
We the kids showed off

[continued]

how we had thrived.
The men, the men.
They were a wonderful lot —
a dentist, a doctor,
a musician, and many an entrepreneur.
They played handball
in the court beyond the tall grass,
and you had to be careful of
copperhead snakes.
Freddy's father caught one
and the doctor skinned it.
Robby's father was a fisherman
who talked of minnows and shiners.
The community comic
was a rotund man named Vic
who once shaved off half his moustache
and proved that few people would notice.
Today I am suddenly taken back
to those bungalow colony days.
My mother has come to visit
with one of her friends from that era.
Like my mother,
these days she lives alone –
like so many of those women.
Where are the men?
The men all died.

UMBRELLA

In the subway car
we are looking glum.
Most of us stare into fluorescent space.
Others pass the time
in The New York Times,
the Daily News, or a paperback.
As I sit paralyzed by
bulky clothes and inertia,
my attention is caught
by the slightly more than middle-aged
black woman on my right.
Glasses perched low on her nose,
she reaches into her plastic tote.
Pulls out a bobbin of thread
and yes, a needle.
Is she really going to try to thread it?
Now I understand, although I am skeptical.
She is going to repair her umbrella.
It's a sad, tired, worn old thing,
its fabric long since parted from its spokes,
whipped about by the wily winds
of city intersections.
By the time we reach Times Square,
she has threaded the needle.
By 23rd Street, she has reattached fabric
to one of the spokes,
is breaking off thread and
preparing to move on to the next.
Before I can censure myself,
I tap her arm and tell her how much

[continued]

I admire her endeavor.
I've often thought of doing that, I confess,
but have never actually done it.
We spend the rest of the ride
making small talk about umbrellas —
lost, found and broken ones —
and the sweet satisfaction of
making repairs.
We laugh about the odds
of her finishing the job
before she reaches her destination.
For this ride at least,
the subway is less cold, less dank,
less menacing.
In fact, after I bid her goodbye,
for the rest of the day
the city seems gentler.

TWO GUITARS

At Sam Ash Guitars,
everyone's a rock star.
Walk in, pick a guitar off a hook,
and plug in to test-drive
one of the dozens of amps
that line the store.
There are so many sounds
booming and bumping into one another,
we can hardly hear the salesperson
who's trying to help us.
My friend the guitar player
makes his selection from the wall.
As his fingers begin to
explore the instrument,
the sounds speak for themselves
and within moments we are taken seriously
and into another room.
Here, one of those wonderful encounters.
An old guy sits down next to us.
Unkempt and toothless.
Holding an instrument
he has selected from the wall,
he starts to play along.
His fingers fumble a lot and there are
more than a few lapses of sound.
But something, somehow, signals
there is real music here.
The kind that was born on backroads
somewhere south and poor.
The kind that's absorbed, not studied.

[continued]

My friend hears it, too,
and instead of ignoring, encourages.
Soon they are deep into dialogue,
picking and strumming,
the old guy humming,
and we've forgotten
it's the middle of the afternoon
at Sam Ash Guitars on West 48th Street
and that in a little while
we'll all go back to our different lives
and try to keep making music
because each of us in our own way
can't live without it.

CHRISTMAS TREES

Lining the the curbs,
piled topsy turvy in green mounds,
tossed out with less respect than garbage,
the Christmas trees comfort each other
as they wait for the trucks
to take them away.
Begone, we are through with you.
These, the same trees that just days ago
stood proud and prized
in places of honor in our homes.
They were the centerpieces
around which our families rallied.
They were our decorated heroes,
symbols of joy,
harboring our treasures
under their protective branches.
They were so important,
we just had to have them
or all would not be right in the world.
Christmas without a tree?
Unthinkable.
Even I, who balks
at their annual appearance
as they're hawked along the streets,
have been known to relent and take one in.
Seeing them now so sad in heaps,
I feel a flash of villain's guilt,
then victim's pain.
How can we value something
so highly one day
and toss it out so brutally the next?

UNCLE ALVIN

In the patch of sun
hitting the bench outside the hotel
where we have all gathered
for Lisa's wedding,
I lay my head on the shoulder
of my favorite uncle,
and let his shoulder warm me
as much as the sun.
In this moment I forget his foibles —
the force of his opinions
and his unrelenting stubbornness.
I remember only
my handsome young bachelor uncle
who taught me as a little girl
about baseball and the Brooklyn Dodgers.
He loved them, so I loved them.
We would discuss Gil and Duke
and their chances of winning the pennant.
He made me feel so special.
And he still does.
To this day, he smiles at me
as if the sight of me lights up his day.
Only one other person
ever smiled at me that way:
my grandmother.
My grandmother is long gone.
Here in the patch of sun,
with ready smile and shoulder,
is Uncle Alvin.

BROWN SUGAR

On normal school days
our breakfast was cold cereal
eaten while reading the backs of the boxes.
But on the few occasions when
mom and dad went on vacation,
grandma and grandpa would stay with us.
Those mornings,
grandma cooked hot cereal,
creamy white farina.
On top she'd put a few clumps of
dark brown sugar
where it would melt and spread.
I'd try to catch a breakaway piece
with each spoonful of cereal,
the sweet brownness of it
mixing with the creamy white stuff,
the whole thing warming me
like grandma's love.
The thing that brings it back to me today
is the taste of brown sugar
dissolving atop a piece of pie
which I've warmed before serving.
The clumps are melting over the walnuts,
lightly glazing the slices of apple.
As I savor each bite,
I experience a pleasure that
goes beyond taste.
I am back in those moments of
grandma's love.
And I'm struck by the thought
that no memories are as powerful as
those evoked by our senses.

MORTALITY

Everyone who died in the last two days
was over 89.
Which is a great relief to me.
Some people check the obituaries
out of morbid curiosity.
Others to see if friends have died.
I check for reassurance.
Telford Taylor, Who
Prosecuted Nazis at Nuremberg,
Is Dead at 90.
Charles D. Webster, 92,
Leader of Garden and Wildlife Groups.
Belle Zeller, 95,
Union Leader and Professor.
My Father, Who
Couldn't Stop Smoking Cigarettes,
Was Dead From Lung Cancer at 66.
I can't imagine life without my mother in it.
It's not that I see her so often.
Or that I depend on her for many things.
But I need to know she's there.
At this writing, she's 83.
So I scan the Times
for evidence of longevity.
Let's see. . . hey!
Lillian Atherford, Researcher and Botanist,
Dies in Her Sleep
in Her Valley Stream, Long Island Home
at 103.

FINGERS

Ten beautiful fingers.
A guitar player.
He lives by those fingers.
Makes them do magic.
I watch in awe as they flex and fly
and pick and strum.
I wonder at the richness
of the sounds that they create.
"This is what I do," he tells me simply.
I sent him to take out the garbage.
In that unfamiliar little room,
where the heavy door
caught him by surprise
and slammed with force across his hand.
He came back in a quiet panic
and spoke in a voice I had never heard.
"Ice. Fast."
I saw his fingers tremble.
Watched the pain and fear on his face.
"They're broken," he said.
"I'm finished."
In those first moments,
as we rallied into action
and immersed his hand in a bowl of ice,
our hearts were immersed in ice as well.
We experienced the implications,
imagined him without his art.
"I'm finished," he repeated.
I soothed and comforted,
forced us both to believe the best.

[continued]

173

"They're not broken," I said.
I wanted to hug him but didn't.
It would have been a sign of defeat.
Finally, like a boat that
appears on the horizon
as two shipwreck survivors await,
the expression on his face relaxed.
"It's okay. I can move them."
The pain lifted.
We treated the cuts.
He held his guitar.
He is whole.
These days,
when he takes out the garbage,
we catch each other's eye.

GRANDMA ANNA

Grandma Anna on my father's side
had 7 children who died on the boat
before she even arrived in America.
The 8th child died soon after
in a hospital in Brooklyn.
When she knew her last child was dying,
Grandma put a gas pipe in her mouth.
A neighbor smelled gas and saved her.
She went to trial.
(Did you know it's illegal to
commit suicide?)
The judge, a sympathetic being,
heard her story and sent her home.
I don't think I inherited the gene
that gave her and Grandpa the courage
to start all over again.
Two more children.
My uncle Sam.
And then my father.
Nobody could give her back the 8 she lost.
But somebody gave her back
another lifetime.
She lived to be 96.

FUNERAL

The women in fashionable black
are chatting outside the
Riverside Memorial Chapel.
The service must be over,
because they're making off
with the flower arrangements
like guests after a wedding.
"At least she came, by God,"
I hear one of them say as I pass.
As opposed to whom, I wonder?
What heartless friend or relative
had not shown up?
I turn to see the faces of these stern judges
trading opinions on this,
someone else's judgment day.
The speaker is a tense, agitated woman,
nervously smoking.
A man is replying
with intense eyes and gestures.
Two young women
at the fringes of the group
are smiling, laughing.
No tears, no dabbing of Kleenex.
A baby has just woken up in its stroller.
A husband pulls up at the curb
and calls out from the car.
We all move on.

FLOWER WOMAN

She must be in her fifties now.
Flower child woman
with skin growing old gently and softly.
Her hair is the same as it was
at Woodstock or wherever it was
she was young:
long and full and straight,
and looking slightly incongruous
now that it's grey.
No makeup.
Full lips.
Calm eyes.
Clothes that snub their nose at fashion.
The things she dropped out of
she dropped for life.
There's beauty here
and it always takes me by surprise.
She wears her aging so unconsciously.
I admire the courage and honesty
of her appearance,
but have to acknowledge
that I find it also appalling.
Seeing her makes me uncomfortably aware
that I am fighting the tide
and she is flowing easily with it.
Do I give her too much credit?
Do I endow her with noble self-acceptance
when it's really simple resignation?
In the end it doesn't matter.
She'd probably no sooner be me
than I would ever be her.

BIRTHDAY CARD

The number sixty
makes me think of speed limits
barely noted as we cruise by
at well above
that many miles per hour.
So, dear David,
I wish you this
as you approach
your sixtieth birthday:
may you regard it
as a mere reference point —
not to limit you in any way,
not to be obeyed,
but acknowledged with a blink
as you continue your journey,
reaching your own number of miles
in your own number of hours
at your own velocity.

JELLY JARS

My grandmother never had drinking glasses.
But nobody ever lacked for
a glass to drink from.
She had the biggest collection
of recycled jelly jars you've ever seen.
Ones with black bands at the top.
Others with red cross-hatched designs.
Some had ridges around the rims
that had once held the cap in place,
and felt funny against your lips
when you drank.
As I kid I got a kick out of them.
My mother picked up the custom,
and all through my childhood,
I don't think I ever drank a glass of milk –
it was always a "jelly jar" of milk.
When I grew up and started earning money,
I started resenting the depression mentality
that continued to keep my mother
from throwing out her jelly jars
and buying a set of glassware.
Maybe this is why
in my house today
there are always lots of drinking glasses.
Whole sets of them that match.
Some clear ones.
Some tinted ones.
Some with stems and
one set of fancy cut crystal.
I'm especially fond of big drinking glasses,

[continued]

really big drinking glasses,
so big that there's not even
a shadow of a doubt
that they ever began life as
jelly jars.

RECYCLING

Someone has gathered
an incredible quantity of bottles and cans.
I almost didn't see him,
bent in on himself,
skin dark and rough,
beard scruffy,
wearing torn layers of salvaged sweaters.
He's got his collection classified:
beer cans, soda cans,
small clear plastic water bottles,
2-liter Coke and Pepsi —
each category bulging inside
a huge recycling sack.
There must be 20 of those bright blue bags
hitched to the frame of a supermarket cart,
bobbling against its sides
as he pushes it slowly down the street,
presumably on his way
to be cashed out for a few dollars.
This is no haphazard scavenger.
This is a man clearly capable.
I can't guess what circumstance
caused him to be out
in this metal-chilling cold,
collecting cans instead of a paycheck.
Surely in better times
he was a productive, if not valued,
member of society.
Isn't there a way to
recycle
this life?

MINK

Anyone who gets the shivers at the
thought of the animals who died
to make a fur coat
should stop reading here.
Anyone who gets the shivers
at the reality of cold,
and I mean deep to the bone
to the point of pain,
when the "real feel" temperature
is 10 degrees,
may understand the fact
that on this frigid day in January
I find myself solo
in the fur department of
Macy's the world's largest store
about to spend a large amount of money
on a mink.
Here I find to my surprise,
not boyfriends and beloveds,
not husbands buying gifts,
not sugar daddies with fat wallets,
but a sisterhood of women
dealing with their emotions
as they treat themselves with
the attention few of them
ever received from anyone else.
Dead animals aside,
this is a beautiful thing.

SUBWAY ADS

"Wait, stop,"
I want to tell the man
sitting across from me on the #2 express.
He's been hooked by the hokum
of a placard above me,
and is writing down the 800-number
of some Dr. Cure-It-All
for hemorrhoids,
poor vision,
bad credit,
or warts.
I am amazed by the gullibility,
the willingness to believe
on the part of people whose difficult lives
I thought would have made them
even more cynical than me.
Less likely to believe
that one simple phone call
will make you rich,
or beautiful,
or free from pain for
the first time in your life.
But that's not the way it works, it seems.
Here's Juan or Jamal or Joe,
copying down the number
and not even embarrassed.
It seems the more we are beaten up,
deceived and disappointed,
the more unabashedly ready we are
to believe in miracles.

WHEELCHAIR

The packed bus pulls up to the curb
where a man in a wheelchair is waiting.
Suddenly,
time shifts into a different gear.
We hear the hiss of escaping air
as the driver sets the brakes.
Flicks some switches.
Gets up and makes his way to the rear.
Raises several seats to create a space.
Presses some buttons
to transform the back steps into a platform.
Lowers it in slow motion to the sidewalk.
Waits while the wheelchair rolls on.
Raises the ramp.
Directs the wheelchair
to the proper position.
Fastens it to the floor.
Lumbers back to the front.
Closes himself back into his space.
Opens the front door for the
people who've been waiting outside.
Are you feeling impatient
reading this description?
Now imagine you've had an awful day,
it's cold,
you're cranky,
and you're late.
I am pleased to say
I have never once
heard anyone complain.

PIGEON

Ifat loves all living creatures.
Whatever the animal,
be it mammal, fish or fowl,
she won't eat it or wear it.
And she can abide no suffering,
no infliction of harm or pain.
I have known this for some time
and am moved by her sincerity,
her kind and caring nature
in everything she does.
But this week she told me about
the pigeon.
A friend had found it,
sick and disabled on a fire escape,
and Ifat went running over
in the middle of night
to take it home and tend to it.
She relates the first days
of gentle force-feeding.
Her search for a vet
who would examine the bird for free.
Her waking from sleep
each time the pigeon ruffled her wings
thinking that something was wrong.
Now each day I ask her,
"how's the pigeon?"
and listen to her heartfelt reports.
I'm struggling with my patterns here.
As a city dweller
I put pigeons and squirrels

[continued]

185

in a category just above mice.
I can't imagine nurturing one.
She is challenging attitudes
I find hard to defend,
but here I stand,
knowing I don't share her concern.
Between tenderness and cruelty
there must be a place
for indifference.
Or is there?
I think I value life.
But as I listen to Ifat,
I realize I don't begin to know.

HONESTY

He woke in the middle of the night
to talk about his troubled conscience.
Twenty dollars in his pocket
that didn't belong to him.
Found on the floor of the deli
where he stood in line
waiting to pay for his coffee.
He had picked up the bill,
thinking it had fallen from his wallet.
Later, counting his money,
he realized it wasn't his.
I, having been on both sides
of a twenty gone astray,
have learned to smile when I find one
and not cry when I lose one.
I'm not equipped to deal with the event
as a moral test.
For him, it was simple and absolute:
It's not mine.
I should not have it.
What should he have done?
Held up a twenty in a New York deli
and asked if anyone had lost it?
Turned it in to the cashier to hold
in the hope that its owner
might return to claim it?
Re-living the scenario with him,
I am unable to suggest a solution.
I have allowed my own honesty
to be compromised in too many ways.

[continued]

Have made too many concessions
to daily life,
too many rationalizations
for less than noble behavior.
I can't believe I'm discussing this
with someone at 3 AM,
not to mention discussing it at all.
Seeing him grapple with his honesty
causes me to examine my own.
I'm not sure where I stand.
But I did think about it.
I guess you could even say
I lost sleep over it.

3,000 DEAD

Two years before the twin towers,
two years before terrorism changed
the way we think forever,
I read this story in The New York Times:
"Reuters reports
at least 3,000 people were killed yesterday
when a powerful earthquake
shook northeastern Afghanistan."
As my hand reached to turn the page,
I stopped.
I tried to take in the reality
of 3,000 people dying.
3,000.
Not apples.
Not dollars.
Those are people.
Three thousand.
The number sat there as words on a page.
I tried to picture 3,000 people.
Everyone who lives on my street?
The total number of people
in my office building?
I thought about the shock and horror
of one person dying a violent death.
Hit by a car,
lying bleeding in the middle of the street.
Or a worker crushed by a crane
at a construction site.
A pedestrian hit by a loose piece of granite.
What did I know of disaster?

[continued]

189

3,000 was too much to take in.
I forced myself to think about just one.
One woman.
Trapped under tons of stone
screaming in vain as rescue workers
search for survivors through rubble.
A person.
One person.
Dead.

PRAYER

I am anxious.
Agitated.
I've worked up my worry
over an early morning appointment
and can't fall asleep.
He tries to soothe me.
I'm aware that I'm acting like a little girl
and he like a father.
Surely remembering his daughter,
he asks if I've said my prayers.
I smile
because I know this is his way.
Quietly,
in his native Portuguese,
he bids me repeat after him.
"Pai nosso . . ."
   "Our father. . ."
"que estaís no ceu. . .
   "who art in heaven. . ."
I follow,
a few words at a time.
I am loving this simple ritual.
"Amém."
Amen.
I close my eyes
and am asleep.

6. FATHER'S DAY

FATHER'S DAY

An annual pause to remember a past
when there was a father for Father's Day.
Your hug and your smile
still travel through time
at the speed of remembrance.
Each year I wonder how you'd look
if you'd lived to this day.
I can't imagine you
small and curved forward
in that old people's way.
To me you are still full and
always just a little too tight around the belt.
I remember many pairs of glasses
each with its own purpose:
one for reading music in the orchestra pit;
one for tinkering with tiny tasks;
one laid aside on the table at tax time.
I see hairy arms in short-sleeved shirts.
I see you putting on fedora and
leaving for work as we, still a family,
finished dessert at the dinner table.
Other images follow,
but they're harder to grasp
as the distance between us grows.
Like remembering a story read long ago.
Or hearing someone else tell me
about their father.
Here's what never fades:
You were your own piece of work.
Stubborn, opinionated,

[continued]

an odd array of foibles set to music.
Today, this year,
I open my self-invented Father's Day card
and find this message:
Thank you for teaching us
how to laugh.

DICTIONARY

On those good days when
we were all together for dinner
and Daddy wasn't sounding off about
someone who had done him wrong,
there was conversation.
And inevitably someone,
either myself or my brother,
would utter a word with a tricky spelling.
Daddy loved words.
And he loved spelling.
"How do you spell that," he'd challenge.
"Don't know," we'd say, "how?"
With a mischievous look, Daddy would say,
"how do you think?"
We'd sigh.
(Why are you torturing us when
you know the answer
and could simply tell us?)
"Try," he'd say.
"We don't know."
"Okay, then go get the dictionary."
Groans.
This meant someone, not Daddy,
had to get up and walk a few feet
to the bookshelf.
"How can we find it in the dictionary
if we don't know how to spell it?"
I don't think he ever answered that,
but it never deflected him.
Before we left that dinner table

[continued]

we'd know how to spell "judgment."
Or the difference between
stationary and stationery.
And a few new vocabulary words
stumbled upon during our search.
Today, as I pull down the "utilities" menu
on my computer,
I wonder how Daddy would have dealt with
Spell Check.

SEÑOR WENCES

My father was
a brilliant, talented, funny man.
He was also disappointed,
depressed,
bitter and angry
for much of the time I remember.
A classical musician by profession,
he was the harshest judge of everyone,
especially himself.
So if someone earned
my father's respect —
when someone's achievements excited him,
made him laugh and come to life,
it must have been someone
very special indeed.
Among this elite group,
immortalized in my mind by
my father's admiration, are:
Prokovieff.
Jascha Heifitz.
Victor Borge.
Kurt Weill.
Ornette Coleman.
And one with no connection to music,
but who struck a special chord
in my father's sense of humor:
Señor Wences.
Oh how we laughed,
the whole family laughed,
at Señor Wences,

[continued]

that eccentric, offbeat ventriloquist
whose silly little fist-characters
were a particularly joyous kind of funny
because my father was laughing.
Señor Wences just died at age 102.
My father died
too
many years ago
at age 66.

PHOTO

A photo of my father,
found in a box in my brother's belongings
just had the startling effect
of making me feel he is back in my life.
I had tossed it onto a table top,
and as I walked by
I felt his presence rise off the paper.
How many years since he died?
How many pangs and cries?
Now here is he,
so exactly the way I remember him,
not looking at me,
but busy with his bassoon.
The lack of eye contact oddly feels right —
perhaps that was part of him and me.
Some camera has captured a moment
never intended to evoke this response,
for this poor portrait in black and white
is clearly a studio pose:
bassoonist with instrument in hand,
fingers on keys, mouth pursed on reed,
looking towards a point in space
I imagine to be the maestro.
"Is this phrasing all right?"
his raised brows seem to ask.
> Yes, I will frame this photo.
> *It's good to see you again.*

PRACTICING

On the sofa near where I sit
Dionísio is practicing,
learning a new piece of music
on the little guitar called a *cavaquinho*.
Over and over he plays the same phrase,
until he can call it his own
and move on.
Some people would find this annoying.
I am surprised to discover
that I find it a comfort.
I realize it reminds me of my father,
who sat in his little room
and tooted his bassoon
while I went about my business
of growing up.
Over and over he played the same phrases
and over the years I learned them too,
hearing those good sounds
of daddy at home
doing his work
and we were a family
or so it sounded.

HUG

I open the door and he's there,
thin lips stretched tight
to form his crescent smile,
belly round but not too big,
firm like a melon tucked into his belt.
I always loved this moment.
Grown child returned to visit,
my father at the door.
This is our hug:
the moment when all our affection
is allowed to be expressed.
We are glad.
The melon belly
makes me lean up into his shoulders
and he makes those silly noises,
grunting like a bear.
I am delighted
at the wind being squeezed out of me.
Homecoming.
Daddy, today I let myself remember,
today I let you into my heart.
All the other days I cannot bear
to think of you —
the pain of loss and longing
leaps to life too readily.
But today I invite your image,
and it doesn't make me cry.
It's Father's Day,
and I, too,
want to celebrate my father.

ASPIRIN

An odd image
out of the many I hold
in the album of my mind:
it was you, my father,
who taught me the secret of
swallowing a pill —
this lesson learned
on the most difficult of all:
that chalky choky miracle called an aspirin.
With deft fingers you carefully positioned
each one on my tongue
(did I really allow this?)
and proved I could then take a gulp
from a glass of water and not gag.
Can any trust be greater
than daughter for father?
How I miss your instruction,
on those occasions
when given so kindly.

HAPPY BIRTHDAY

Your birthday again,
dear father.
Another year, not of life,
but of memories moving further back
like the distance since your death.
Images that over the years
have sifted themselves,
leaving only strange residue
that makes no rhyme or reason.
I close my eyes as if making a wish
and the candles that light my mind are:
Your retreat to the bathroom after dinner
to smoke your cigarette.
And I suspect,
to get away from us all still at the table.
Your lifelong quest
to make science of the imperfect art
of making reeds for your bassoon.
The sound of that bassoon as you practiced,
always beginning with the notes
that to me became your voice,
that little riff from the Mozart concerto.
Your refusal to ever answer a question
in the belief that we must first try
to figure it out for ourselves.
The many April 15ths
with you sitting amidst papers and receipts
at the dining room table,
your nose indented with the impression of
the eyeglasses lying before you on the table.

[continued]

Your boxer shorts and undershirt
(did you really wear them all day
when you were home,
my father?)
Your sense of humor.
It saved us all.
These are the candles
that light my mind on your birthday
as I stop and take a few moments
to wish you . . .
were here.

Alphabetical Index